영어문화권 문하생을 지도하는 태권도 지도자,
해외 취업, 해외 봉사활동 또는 시범단 활동을
하는 태권도 전공자를 위한 태권도 영어 지도서

태권도 코칭 실무 영어
Coaching Taekwondo in English

고 봉 수 · 김 동 원 공저

대경북스

저|자|소|개

고 봉 수

원광대학교 대학원 이학박사
1996 월드컵태권도선수권대회 국가대표코치 역임
2009 세계태권도품새선수권대회 한국대표코치 역임
2010 대한민국 체육훈장 기린장 수상
현 전주비전대학교 태권도체육학과 교수
    세계태권도문화엑스포 조직위원회 사무총장
    2017 무주 WTF세계태권도선수권대회 조직위원회 경기지원본부장
    전라북도태권도협회 상임부회장
    대한태권도협회 도장특별위원회 위원
    2017 국기원 자격검정위원회 위원

김 동 원

서강대학교 독어독문학과 졸업
라크로스 위스콘신대학교 스포츠행정학석사
성균관대학교 대학원 체육학박사
세한대학교 생활체육학과 태권도 전공영어 강사
명지대학교 바둑학과 강사
현 명지대학교 사회교육원 바둑학과 객원교수
    서울시립대학교 평생교육원 초빙교수

자|세|감|수 및 시|범

서 영 애

태권도 공인8단
체육훈장 맹호장 수상
2006~2014 세계태권도품새선수권대회 8회 우승

권 형 남

2010 세계태권도품새선수권대회 한국대표팀 코치
2013 세계태권도품새선수권대회 태국대표팀 코치
2016 아시아태권도품새선수권대회 금메달
국기원 세계태권도연수원(WTA) 품새 강사

태권도 코칭 실무 영어

초판인쇄 2017년 6월 15일
초판발행 2017년 6월 20일
발 행 인 민유정
발 행 처 대경북스
  ISBN 978-89-5676-598-3

등록번호 제 1-1003호
서울시 강동구 천중로42길 45(길동 379-15) 2F
전화: (02)485-1988, 485-2586~87 · 팩스: (02)485-1488
e-mail: dkbooks@chol.com · http://www.dkbooks.co.kr

Testimonial 추천의 글

World Taekwondo Federation has held an inaugural assembly with 35 representatives from 19 nations in Kukkiwon (World Taekwondo Headquarters) in 1973, straight after the first World Taekwondo Championship.

World Taekwondo Federation was founded to properly propagate Taekwondo globally, with its distinct spirit. Which is to say, that we set our goals on contributing to peace on mankind through Taekwondo, and on globalization of Taekwondo and technical development of Taekwondo.

Chung-Won Choue
(President of WTF)

World Taekwondo Federation currently stands as a global organization, with organizations that manage each nation's Taekwondo depending on its continent as members. We have 208 members from 5 continents around the world.

Taekwondo is now a global sport, worthy of the name, and is at a crucial point where it is to improve not only on its quantity, but also on its quality.

It is only the perfect timing to publish an English manual for Taekwondo coaching. We believe that this is the first book that aims to guide through practical English for Taekwondo coaching.

We can only imagine the distress that the writers may have encountered in writing this book. We express our deepest gratitude for the writers' continual patience and effort that bound this book. We hope 'Coaching Taekwondo in English' acts as a great manual for those Taekwondo leaders that strive for globalization of Taekwondo.

Furthermore, we look forward to more publications on practical Taekwondo and studies on Taekwondo in various fields with the publication of 'Practical English for Taekwondo Coaching'.

June 2017

세계태권도연맹은 제1회 세계태권도선수권대회 직후인 1973년에 국기원에서 19개국 대표 35명이 참가한 가운데 창립총회를 가졌습니다.

세계태권도연맹의 설립 목적은 고유의 정신과 더불어 태권도를 전 세계적으로 올바르게 보급시키는 데 있습니다. 즉 태권도를 통한 인류평화, 태권도의 세계화, 태권도 경기의 발달, 태권도 기술개발 등에 이바지하는 것을 목표로 하는 것입니다.

현재 세계태권도연맹은 세계적인 기구로 대륙별 각 나라의 태권도를 관할하는 기구를 그 회원으로 하며, 전 세계 5개 대륙에 208개의 회원국을 두고 있습니다.

이제 태권도는 명실상부한 세계인의 스포츠로 양적 성장뿐만 아니라 질적 성장을 도모하는 중요한 시점에 와 있습니다.

이러한 시점에서 태권도 지도를 주 목적으로 하는 영어로 된 지도서의 출간은 시의적절하다 할 수 있습니다. 교본이 아닌 순수하게 지도를 목적으로 하는 실무적인 태권도 영어 지도서는 이 책이 처음이 아닌가 싶습니다.

책의 집필과정에서 저자분들이 겪었을 고충이 눈에 선합니다. 오랜 인내와 노력을 통해 책을 완성한 저자분들의 노고에 깊은 감사를 드리면서, 『태권도 코칭 실무 영어』가 태권도의 세계화를 위해 노력하는 많은 지도자들에게 좋은 지침서가 될 수 있기를 바랍니다.

또한 본 서의 출간을 계기로 다양한 방면으로의 태권도 연구와 영어로 된 태권도 실무 서적의 출판이 활발해지기를 기대해봅니다.

2017년 6월

세계태권도연맹 총재　　조 정 원

Chungwon Choue

Testimonial 추천의 글

After the first step forward as World's first Taekwondo Headquarters in 1972, Kukkiwon have strived to develop Taekwondo culture through the growth in Taekwondo spirit and accession of techniques. Also, we have contributed to peace for mankind with global propagation of Taekwondo.

Hyun-Deuk Oh
(President of Kukkiwon)

During the 45 or more years that passed, Taekwondo was spread globally in the name of 'Korean Wave', and more global neighbors started recognizing Taekwondo. To participate in such time stream, Kukkiwon has established World Taekwondo Academy (WTA) in 1983 and educated and produced 140,000 refined Taekwondo leaders with professional knowledge to strive to disseminate the spirit and technique of Taekwondo into the world.

Until now, in producing Taekwondo leaders, we have suffered obstacles of communication difficulties in globalizing of Taekwondo. In regards to this matter, we cannot seize to express our delight in encountering the news that 'Coaching Taekwondo in English', a manual for teaching practical English for Taekwondo, is to be published.

We believe that this manual will become a great help to not only those Taekwondo leaders that coach domestically, but also to those who desire to coach overseas. We would like to send our applause for the writers' passion and effort, and also look forward to seeing various researches and academic attempts for globalization of Taekwondo to be performed.

We ask for your continuous attention and support on Kukkiwon (World Taekwondo Headquarters), and may there be good health and happiness in your family.

June 2017

국기원은 지난 1972년 세계 최초의 태권도 본부로 첫 발을 내딛은 이래, 그 동안 태권도 정신과 기술의 계승 및 발전을 통한 태권도 문화 창달에 힘써왔습니다. 또한 세계적인 태권도의 전파와 보급을 통하여 인류평화에 기여해 왔습니다.

45년여의 세월이 흐르는 동안 태권도는 '한류'라는 이름으로 세계에 전파되었고, 태권도에 대한 세계 이웃들의 관심도 높아졌습니다. 이러한 시대적 흐름에 동참하고자 국기원은 1983년부터 세계태권도지도자연수원(WTA)을 개원개원하여 전문적인 지식과 소양을 갖춘 14만 명의 지도자를 양성·배출함으로써, 세계속에 태권도의 정신과 기술을 올바르게 보급시키는 데 매진하고 있습니다.

그 동안 태권도 지도자 양성 과정에서 언어소통의 문제는 태권도 세계화의 걸림돌로 대두되곤 하였습니다. 바로 이 문제를 해결하기 위하여 태권도의 실무를 영어로 가르치는 지도서인 『태권도 코칭 실무 영어』를 발간한다는 소식에 반가움을 금할 수 없습니다.

이 지도서는 태권도의 신체 사용 부위와 기본동작, 품새 및 겨루기를 포함하며, 호신술과 시범에 대한 내용을 망라하고 있어, 국내에서 활동하는 태권도 지도자들은 물론, 해외에서 활동하고자 하는 태권도 전공자에게 큰 도움이 되리라 생각합니다. 아울러 저자분들의 노력과 열정에 박수를 보내며, 앞으로 태권도의 세계화를 위한 다양한 연구와 학문적인 시도가 이루어지기를 기대합니다.

앞으로도 세계 태권도본부 국기원에 대한 지속적인 관심과 성원을 부탁드리며, 여러분 모두의 건승과 가정에 행복이 충만하시기를 기원합니다.

2017년 6월

국기원 원장 오 현 득

Testimonial 추천의 글

Taekwondo was born in a form of martial arts with characteristics of Korean race, in the ancient time where Korea was made out of tribes. In the era of Three Kingdoms, it was named Taekkyeon and Subak in the process of improvement, and was righted as systemized martial arts of 'Subakhee' in the Koryo Dynasty.

Chang-Shin Choi
(President of KTA)

After overcoming the dark period of Japanese Colonial Era, people gathered to train the young generation to recover the forgotten Taekwondo, established Korea Taekwondo Association(KTA) in 1961, joined Korean Olympic Committee as a member organization in 1963, and finally, got Taekwondo adopted as an official sport in the 44th National Sports Festival. Taekwondo has gone through an impressive improvement then on, and today, we are able to witness the proud match of Taekwondo in the Olympics, the festival of humankind.

Our Taekwondo is now at a crucial point in taking a new leap toward globalization. Our Taekwondo Leaders are now burdened with the assignment of overcoming the language barrier to catch up with globalization of Taekwondo.

And then we came across the news that 'Coaching Taekwondo in English', the English manual for Taekwondo, was to be published. There is an increase in English speaking pupils, and Taekwondo related employment and voluntary service opportunities and demonstration crew are becoming more and more active. It couldn't be better if our Taekwondo experts could coach and spread Taekwondo skillfully in English at this time.

We express our deepest gratitude for the hard work that the writers have poured in to produce such a wonderful manual at such wonderful time. We hope that 'Coaching Taekwondo in English' becomes a sturdy steppingstone for Taekwondo's globalization.

June 2017

태권도는 고대 부족국가시대부터 한민족 고유의 무술 형태로 생성되었으며, 삼국시대에 이르러 택견, 수박 등으로 불리우며 발전되다가 고려시대에 이르러 수박희라는 체계화된 무예로 정립되었습니다.

일제강점기의 암흑기를 지나 해방 이후 잊혀진 우리의 태권도를 되찾기 위해 뜻있는 이들이 모여 후진을 양성하기 시작하여, 1961년에 대한태권도협회를 창설하고, 1963년에 대한체육회에 가맹단체로 가입하였으며, 제44회 전국체전에 태권도가 공식경기로 채택되었습니다. 그 뒤 태권도는 눈부신 발전을 이루었고 오늘날에는 인류의 제전인 올림픽 무대에서 자랑스러운 태권도의 모습을 볼 수 있게 되었습니다.

이제 우리의 태권도는 세계화, 국제화를 위해 도약하는 중요한 시점에 와 있습니다. 태권도의 국제화에 발맞추기 위해 우리 태권도 지도자들은 언어의 장벽을 극복해야 한다는 과제를 안고 있습니다.

이러한 시점에 태권도 영어 지도서인『태권도 코칭 실무 영어』의 발간 소식을 듣게 되었습니다. 영어문화권 문하생들이 크게 늘어나고 있고, 태권도 관련 해외 취업과 봉사활동, 시범단 활동이 점점 활발해지고 있는 지금의 상황에서 태권도 전공자들이 능숙하게 영어로 태권도를 지도하고 알려나갈 수 있다면 더할 나위 없이 좋을 것입니다.

적절한 시기에 공들여 좋은 교재를 만들어 주신 저자분들의 노고에 감사드리며,『태권도 코칭 실무 영어』가 태권도의 세계화와 국제화를 위한 디딤돌 역할을 할 수 있기를 기대해 봅니다.

2017년 6월

대한태권도협회 회장　최 창 신

Introduction 머리말

Taekwondo is Korea's representative martial arts, and it is a globally spread sports of one-on-one matches, and it is Korea's national sports. It is an educationally beneficial sports that plants healthy values and patriotism in young Koreans' heart and leads to completion of self.

Taekwondo has become an international sports, worthy of its name, in all forms of international competitions. It has enhanced national prestige, being chosen as a formal game in Olympic Games. Behind all these achievements, there were passion, patience and effort of those leaders that has spread Taekwondo overseas over a long time.

Taekwondo is at the point where it is waiting to become international sports. At this point we feel the need of researching and developing standardized English expressions and unifying and establishing unified English expressions for Taekwondo.

To satisfy this need, we have comet o produce an English manual for Taekwondo in the name of 'Coaching Taekwondo in English'. We have proceeded with writing focusing on the goal, that English coaching for not only Taekwondo's principle, positions, basic moves and techniques, but also its defensive moves and in learning to coach, to become possible.

We hope this becomes a good manual for those Taekwondo majors who are coaching English speaking pupils, looking for international employment or voluntary services, and for those who are coaching Taekwondo.

Finally, we would like to express our deepest thanks to coaches Young-ae Seo and Hyeong-nam Kwon, who have demonstrated the moves for photo shooting and put in hard work to correctly translate Taekwondo terms, and also their students who modeled for the movement photo shooting.

June 2017

태권도는 대표적인 한민족 고유의 무술로서 세계적으로 널리 보급된 투기 스포츠이자 대한민국의 국기입니다. 또한 태권도는 자라나는 어린이와 청소년에게 건전한 가치관과 애국심을 심어주며, 자아완성으로 이끌어주는 좋은 교육적 수단이기도 합니다.

오늘날 태권도는 명실상부한 국제 스포츠종목이 되어 다양한 형태의 국제대회가 개최되고 있으며, 특히 올림픽 정식종목으로서 채택되어 국위를 선양하고 있습니다. 이와 같은 성과 뒤에는 오랜 시간에 걸쳐 태권도를 해외에 보급해 온 지도자들의 열정, 인내, 그리고 노력이 있었습니다.

이제 태권도는 세계인의 스포츠로 발전하기 위해 도약하는 시점에 서 있습니다. 지금의 상황에서 우리는 태권도를 영어로 올바르게 표현하는 표준화된 방법을 연구 개발하여 국제적으로 통일된 태권도 영어를 정립해야 할 필요성을 느낍니다.

이러한 시대적 요구에 부응하고자 부족하나마 태권도 영어 지도서를 기획하고 『태권도 코칭 실무 영어』라는 제목으로 출판하게 되었습니다. 태권도의 원리와 자세, 기본동작, 품새는 물론 호신술과 시범단 활동에 이르기까지 태권도의 전반적인 실무를 영어로 지도할 수 있도록 하는 데 목표를 두고 집필작업을 진행했습니다.

아무쪼록 이 책이 영어문화권 문하생을 지도하는 태권도 지도자, 해외 취업, 해외 봉사활동, 시범단 활동 등을 하는 태권도 전공자들에게 좋은 지침서가 되기를 바랍니다.

끝으로 사진 촬영을 위해 자세 교정 및 품새 시범을 직접 해주시고 용어의 교열 작업을 위해 애써주신 서영애, 권형남 두 사범님과 태권도 동작 촬영을 위해 모델이 되어 준 학생들에게 고마움을 전합니다.

2017년 6월

Table of Contents

Part 1. Parts of the Body in Taekwondo
태권도의 신체 사용 부위

Part 2. Basic Movements of Taekwondo
태권도의 기본동작

Part 3. Poomsae
품새

Part 4. Kyorugi
겨루기

Part 5. Self-Defense
호신술

Part 6. Taekwondo Demonstration Group
태권도시범단

Supplement
부록

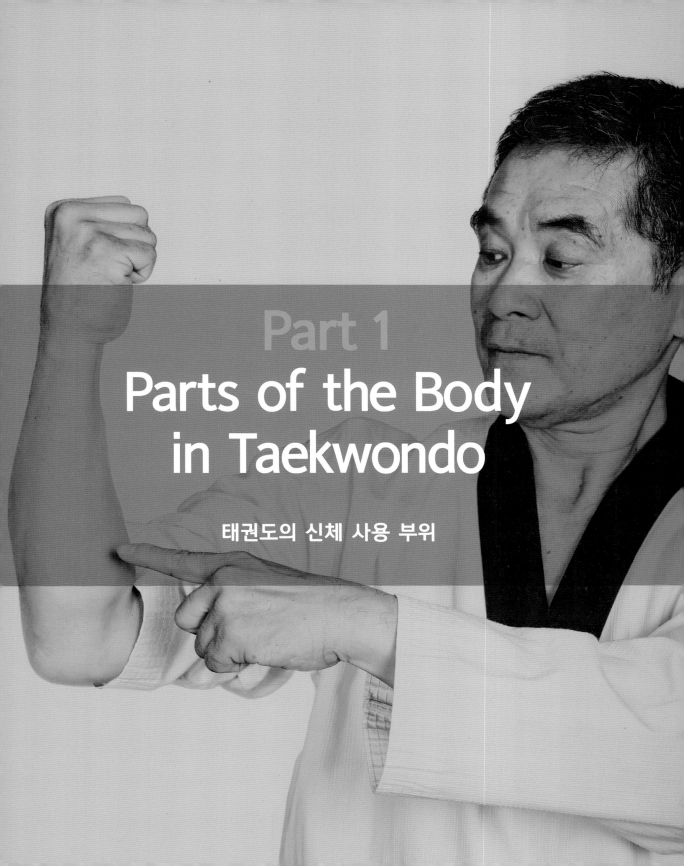

Part 1
Parts of the Body
in Taekwondo

태권도의 신체 사용 부위

Master   Hello, everyone! Nice to meet you all. This is your instructor and we will exercise together for one year.

Disciple   Yes, master. Good to meet you.

Master   From now on, I will try to teach you Taekwondo easily and interestingly so please trust and follow me positively.

Disciple   Of course. Please guide us well then.

Master   Today, we will first learn about all the applicable parts of the human body.

Basically, all parts of the body are used for attack (offense) and defense in Taekwondo.

In executing Taekwondo techniques, power comes from the trunk.

However, the arms and legs are used to attack the target parts of the opponent's body.

At this moment, the hands and the feet play the key roles.

사범	여러분 안녕하세요, 만나서 반갑습니다. 오늘부터 1년간 여러분과 같이 수련하게 될 사범입니다.

문하생 네, 사범님. 만나게 되어 반갑습니다.

사범 앞으로 여러분이 태권도를 쉽고 즐겁게 배울 수 있도록 노력할 것이니 저를 믿고 적극적으로 따라 주시기 바랍니다.

문하생 네, 앞으로 잘 부탁드리겠습니다.

사범 오늘은 먼저 신체의 사용부위에 대해 알아보겠습니다.

기본적으로 태권도는 공격과 방어를 위해 온몸을 사용합니다.

태권도 기술을 수행할 때 힘은 몸통에서 나옵니다.

그런데 상대방 신체의 목표 부위를 공격하기 위해서 팔과 다리가 사용됩니다.

이러한 공격 순간에 손과 발이 결정적인 역할을 하게 됩니다.

Words

instructor 사범, 강사
attack 공격
offense 공격
defense 방어
trunk 몸통
opponent 상대, 적
face 얼굴
bottom 아래, 바닥

Expressions

from now on 앞으로, 지금부터
learn about~ ~에 대해 알아보다, 배우다
comes from~ ~에서 나오다, ~로부터 오다
play the key roles 결정적인 역할을 하다

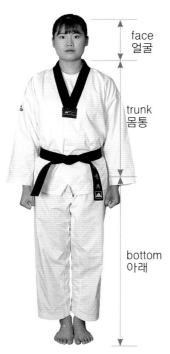

face
얼굴

trunk
몸통

bottom
아래

The parts of the body

Target of the body are mainly classified as three main parts; face, trunk, and bottom which is the lower part of the body.

Specifically, eight parts of fist, hand, wrist, forearm, elbow, foot, shin, and knee are used for both offense and defense.

Let me introduce these three target parts and eight specific body parts to you one by one in each class.

1. Face

Master   The face is the first part that we need to know.

The face refers to the front of head, located between the forehead(brow) to lower jaw and between two ears.

2. Trunk

Master   As the central part of the body, the trunk is the primary part excluding face, the neck, and leg.

공격 목표 부위는 크게 '얼굴', '몸통', 그리고 신체의 아래 부분인 '아래' 세 부분으로 구분됩니다.

구체적으로 공격 및 방어에 사용하는 부위들에는 주먹, 손, 팔목, 팔뚝, 팔꿈치(팔굽), 발, 정강이, 무릎의 여덟 가지가 있습니다.

저는 앞으로 매 수업시간마다 이러한 세 가지 공격 목표 부위와 여덟 가지 구체적인 신체부위들에 대해 순차적으로 자세히 소개해 드리겠습니다.

1. 얼굴

사범 처음으로 알아야할 부위는 얼굴입니다.

얼굴은 머리의 정면을 말하며, 이마로부터 아래턱에 이르는 양쪽 귀 사이에 있는 부분을 말합니다.

2. 몸통

사범 몸통은 신체의 중심 부분으로서 일반적으로 얼굴, 목, 다리를 제외한 주요 부위를 말합니다.

3. Bottom, The Lower Part of the Body

Master   The lower part of the trunk is called 'the bottom' and includes the abdomen, groin, thigh, knee, shin, ankle, and foot.

4. Fist

Master   A fist is formed by clenching the fingers.

The fist in Taekwondo is a simple form of fists clenching the fingers firmly folding into the palm.

Here, only the joint parts of the first(index) finger and middle finger are used for punching techniques.

The way of forming starts from the unfolded palm of the hand.

Everyone follow me, please. First, start fingertips to clench up to the first finger joints until the fingernails aren't visible.

Then, clench the first(index) and middle fingers with the thumb.

The fist

3. 아래

사범   몸통 아래 부분을 '아래'라고 부르며, 복부, 사타구니, 허벅지, 무릎, 정강이, 발목, 그리고 발이 포함됩니다.

4. 주먹

사범   주먹은 손가락을 오므려 꽉 쥔 모양을 말합니다.

태권도에서 주먹은 손가락을 손바닥쪽을 향해 접어서 꽉 쥔 모양을 말합니다.

이때 집게손가락과 가운데손가락의 결합 부분만이 지르기 기술에 사용됩니다.

주먹 쥐는 법은 손바닥을 편 상태에서 시작합니다.

자, 여러분들도 같이 따라하시죠. 먼저 손가락을 접기 시작하여 손가락 첫 번째 마디까지 손톱이 보이지 않도록 쥐어보세요.

다음으로 엄지손가락으로 집게손가락과 가운데손가락을 감싸면 됩니다.

Words
abdomen 복부
groin 사타구니
thigh 허벅지
knee 무릎
shin 정강이
ankle 발목
foot 발
clench 꽉 쥐다
unfold 펴다
fingertip 손끝
fingernail 손톱
index finger 검지, 집게손가락
thumb 엄지

Expressions
be formed by~ ~로 이루어지다
be used for~ ~로 사용되다
start from~ ~에서 시작되다
get invisible 보이지 않게 되다

In Taekwondo, the fist is usually applied to the punch techniques and some precautions are as follows;

The fist should not be bent at the wrist.

Both the Hand Back and forearm should be kept on a straight line.

Also, the Hand Back and the first-joints of the clenched fingers should form a right angle.

Its forms are classified into five main types according to its usage: Back Fist, Hammer Fist, Flat Fist, Knuckle Protruding Fist and Pincers Fist.

 ### 4.1 Back Fist

Master   The shape of the Back Fist is the same as a simple fist but the only difference is its usage.

That is, the back of the fist is used for attacks.

4.2 Hammer Fist

Master   The shape of the Hammer Fist is the same as a simple fist, but this time only the little finger side is used for attacks.

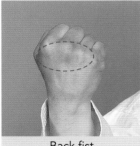

Back fist

Hammer fist

태권도에서 주먹은 대개 지르기 기술에 사용되며, 몇 가지 주의사항은 다음과 같습니다.

주먹은 팔목에서 꺾이게 쥐지 말아야 합니다.

그리고 손등과 팔뚝이 일직선이 되어야 합니다.

또한 손등과 굽힌 손가락의 첫마디가 직각을 이뤄야 합니다.

주먹의 형태는 사용법에 따라 다섯 가지로 분류 됩니다 : 등주먹, 메주먹, 편주먹, 밤주먹, 집게주먹

Words

precaution 주의사항
hand back 손등
forearm 팔뚝
back fist 등주먹
hammer fist 메주먹
flat fist 편주먹
knuckle protruding fist 밤주먹
pincers fist 집게주먹

Expressions

be formed by~ ~로 이루어지다
be used for~ ~로 사용되다
start from~ ~에서 시작되다
get invisible 보이지 않게 되다

4.1 등주먹

사범 등주먹의 모양은 보통의 주먹과 같고, 단지 쓰임새만 다를 뿐입니다.

즉, 주먹의 등이 공격에 사용되는 것이죠.

4.2 메주먹

사범 메주먹의 모양은 보통주먹과 같습니다. 그런데 이번에는 새끼손가락의 옆부분만이 공격에 사용됩니다.

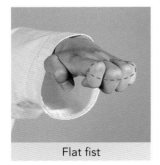

Flat fist

4.3 Flat Fist

Master   At a clenched simple fist, the Flat Fist is formed by standing the first joints of four fingers except for the thumb.

The foremost point of Flat Fist is that the second joints of fingers are used for attack.

For this reason, it reaches longer than the simple fist so that it can deliver a stronger attack.

Like a fist, a Flat Fist is used as one of the punch techniques, but sometimes it can be also used in scratching the target.

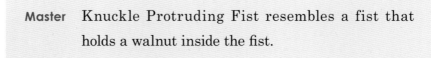

4.4 Knuckle Protruding Fist

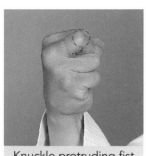

Knuckle protruding fist

Master   Knuckle Protruding Fist resembles a fist that holds a walnut inside the fist.

To have a closer look, the second joint of the middle finger protrudes.

This middle finger is put forward by keeping the first joint slightly bent down and the third joint is supported by the thumb inside the fist.

4.3 편주먹

사범 주먹을 쥔 상태에서 엄지손가락을 제외한 모든 손가락의 첫 번째 관절을 똑바로 세우면 편주먹이 됩니다.

편주먹에서 가장 중요한 점은 손가락의 두 번째 마디가 공격에 사용된다는 것입니다.

이 때문에 보통주먹보다 조금 더 목표물에 닿을 수 있어 보다 강한 타격을 가할 수 있습니다.

주먹과 같이 편주먹은 지르기 기술의 하나로 사용됩니다. 그러나 때때로 목표물을 훑을 때 사용되기도 합니다.

4.4 밤주먹

사범 밤주먹은 보통주먹과 같은 모양입니다. 그런데 주먹 안에 호두를 쥐고 있는 것처럼 보입니다.

자세히 살펴보면 가운데손가락의 두 번째 관절이 돌출되어 있습니다.

이 가운데손가락은 첫 번째 관절을 약간 아래로 굽히고 세 번째 관절이 주먹 안에 있는 엄지손가락에 의해 받쳐지게 된 것입니다.

Words
erect 세우다
foremost 가장 중요한, 맨 앞에 위치한
scratch 훑다
resemble 같다, 닮다
walnut 호두
protrude 돌출되다, 튀어나오다

Expressions
except ~ ~을 제외하고
be used for ~ ~로 사용되다
longer than ~ ~보다 긴
have a good look 잘 살펴보다
bent down 굽히다

The second joint of the middle finger is used in the punch attack, but pierces are deeper than the fist in that they are used like lethal weapons.

4.5 Pincers Fist

Master   The last type is the Pincers Fist.

Pincers fist

The thumb and first(index) finger are held open apart from each other when the other three fingers are being clenched.

Here, both the thumb and first(index) finger forming like an arc hand shape playing the role of pincers.

And, at punch techniques, the two pincer fingers grasp and tear off the target.

It is generally used to punch the throat and simultaneously hackle it with the tips of two pincer fingers.

가운데손가락의 두 번째 관절이 지르기 공격에 사용됩니다. 그런데 보통주먹보다 더 깊이 찌르게 되어 치명적인 무기처럼 쓰입니다.

Words

pierce 찌르다
lethal weapon 치명적인 무기
arc hand shape 아금손 모양
grasp 꽉잡다, 움켜쥐다
tear off 떼어내다
throat 인후, 목구멍
simultaneously 동시에
hackle 위해를 가하다

4.5 집게주먹

사범 마지막 모양은 집게주먹입니다.

엄지손가락과 집게손가락은 서로 떨어진 채로 벌려져 있고, 다른 세 손가락은 보통주먹에서와 같이 말려 있습니다.

여기에서 아금손 모양을 한 엄지손가락과 집게손가락이 집게의 역할을 합니다.

Expressions

open apart 벌려져 있다
each other 서로
play the role 역할을 하다

그리고 지르기 기술에서 그 집게 역할의 두 손가락이 목표물을 꽉 잡고 공격합니다.

집게주먹은 일반적으로 인후 부위를 지르거나 동시에 집게 역할을 하는 도 손가락으로 인후 부위를 공격합니다.

5. Hand

Master   The basic form of Taekwondo hand is a little bit different from the normal one in our every day life.

The hand in Taekwondo means an open hand with its fingers slightly bent at their third joints.

Therefore, its applicable parts double those of the fist and vary according to the targets.

5.1 Hand Blade

Master   To form the Hand Blade, first stick the four fingers side by side, keeping their last joints bent inward slightly.

Hand blade

Then, attach the thumb to the first joint area of the index finger.

Here, the thumb could also be slightly bent at the first joint.

The Hand Blade uses the little finger side from its first joint down to the wrist.

5. 손

사범   태권도에서 기본적인 손의 모양은 일상에서의 모습과는 약간 다르게 합니다.

태권도에 있어 손은 세 번째 마디만 약간 굽힌 펼친 손 모양을 말합니다.

따라서 손의 사용 가능한 부위는 주먹의 두 배에 해당하며, 목표물에 따라 달라질 수 있습니다.

5.1 손날

사범   손날 형태를 갖추려면 먼저 마지막 마디를 안쪽으로 약간 굽히고 네 손가락을 서로 가지런히 붙입니다.

그리고 나서 엄지손가락을 집게손가락의 첫 번째 마디 부분에 갖다 붙입니다.

이때 엄지손가락도 첫 번째 마디에서 약간 굽혀지게 합니다.

손날에서는 새끼손가락의 측면을 그것의 첫 번째 마디부터 팔목까지 사용하게 됩니다.

Words

joint 관절
applicable 사용 가능한
stick 붙이다
wrist 팔목

Expressions

a little bit 약간
according to ~에 따라
side by side 가지런히
bend inward 안쪽으로 굽히다

The Hand Blade is used for both hitting and blocking techniques.

In Hand Blade, the hand must be kept in a straight line with the forearm.

Also its form should not be bent either upward, downward, inward nor outward.

5.2 Hand Blade Back

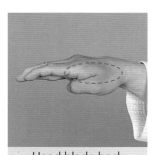

Hand blade back

Master Hand Blade Back has the same form with Hand Blade, but the thumb is deeply buried inside the palm.

In Hand Blade Back, the side of the first joints of both the thumb and index finger are applicable.

And it is used in hitting and blocking techniques.

Here, you should keep the thumb buried deeply into the palm.

5.3-5.5 5.3 Hand Back, Back of the Hand

Master Hand Back has the same form of Hand Blade, but Hand Back may keep the fingers relatively loose.

그리고 손날은 치기와 막기 기술에서 사용합니다.

손날에서 손은 반드시 팔뚝과 동일선상에 있어야 합니다.

또한 손날의 형태는 위, 아래, 안팎으로 굽혀지면 안 됩니다.

5.2 손날등

사범 손날등은 손날과 같은 모양이나 엄지손가락이 손바닥 안쪽으로 깊이
들어가 있는 점이 다릅니다.

손날등에서는 엄지손가락과 집게손가락의 첫 번째 마디 옆부분을 사
용하게 됩니다.

그리고 치기와 막기 기술에 사용됩니다.

여기에서 엄지손가락이 손바닥으로 깊이 들어가야 함을 잊지 말아야
합니다.

5.3 손등

사범 손등은 손날과 같은 모양인데요, 다만 손가락을 조금 더 느슨하게 해
도 됩니다.

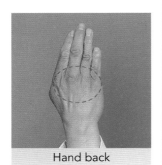

Hand back

It uses all parts of the hand from the finger's back to Hand Back.

This is used mainly as a hit technique for a momentary attack at a close distance.

At the moment of attack, the wrist part must accompany a repulsive reaction to hand back.

5.4 Flat Hand Tips

Master Flat Hand Tips are the same as the form of Hand Blade.

However, especially the first(index) finger, middle finger and ring finger are tightly attached side by side with their fingertips straightened in a line.

The fingertips of the above mentioned three fingers.

This is mainly used in the thrusting technique but also applicable to the hackling technique.

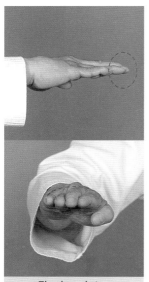

Flat hand tips

5.5 Scissors' Hand Tips

Master At Scissors Hand Tips, the index finger and middle

손등은 손가락끝부터 손등까지 모든 부위를 사용하게 됩니다.

이것은 주로 가까운 거리에서 순간적인 공격을 가할 때 치기 기술로 사용됩니다.

공격하는 순간에 팔목에서부터 손등을 튕기는 것과 같은 동작을 같이 해주어야 합니다.

5.4 편손끝

사범   편손끝은 손날의 형태와 같습니다.

그러나 특히 집게손가락, 가운데손가락, 반지손가락(약지)이 일자로 늘어선 채로 손끝이 서로 밀착되어 있는 점이 다릅니다.

위에서 설명한 세 손가락의 끝이 사용됩니다.

편손끝은 주로 찌르기 기술에 사용되지만 훑기 기술에도 사용됩니다.

5.5 가위손끝

사범   가위손끝에서는 집게손가락과 가운데손가락이 서로 떨어진 채로 뻗

Words

momentary attack 순간적인 공격
accompany 동반하다, 동행하다
repulsive reaction 튕겨주는 동작
first(index) finger 검지(둘째)손가락
middle finger 가운데손가락(중지)
ring finger 반지손가락(약지)
especially 특히
tightly 단단히, 꽉
thrust 찌르다, 밀다

Expressions

used mainly 주로 사용되다
at a close distance 가까운 거리에서
At the moment of ~를 하는 순간에
above mentioned 위에서 이야기한
applicable to ~에 사용되다

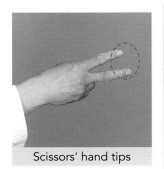

Scissors' hand tips

finger are stretched with the fingers opened apart from each other.

And the ring finger and little finger are rolled into the palm, the second joint of the ring finger supported by the thumb.

The fingertips of both the first(index) and middle finger are used, applying usually to thrusting techniques for attacking the opponent's eyes.

 5.6 Single Hand Tip

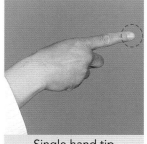

Single hand tip

Master To form the Single Hand Tip, first keep the first (index) finger stretched to look as if it points at something.

This time the thumb powerfully supports the second joint of the bent middle finger.

Here, only the tip of the first(index) finger is used and mainly applied to thrusting into one of the opponent's eyes and able to stab other vital parts.

5.7 Combined(Joint) Two Hand Tips

Master To form the Combined Two Hand Tips, make the stretched first(index) finger overlapped by the

어져 있습니다.

그리고 반지손가락(약지)과 새끼손가락이 손바닥쪽으로 말려 있으며, 엄지손가락은 반지손가락의 두 번째 마디를 받치고 있습니다.

집게와 가운데손가락끝이 사용되며, 주로 상대방의 양쪽 눈을 공격하기 위한 찌르기 기술에 이용됩니다.

5.6 한손끝

사범 한손끝을 만들려면 먼저 집게손가락을 무언가를 가리키는 것처럼 쭉 뻗게 하세요.

이번에 엄지손가락은 굽혀진 가운데손가락의 두 번째 마디를 강하게 지탱하게 됩니다.

여기에서는 집게손가락끝만 사용되며, 상대방의 눈을 찌르기할 때 사용 가능하며, 기타 주요부위를 찌를 수 있습니다.

5.7 모은두손끝

사범 모은두손끝은 가운데손가락을 뻗은 집게손가락에 올려 겹치고 다른 손가락들은 가위손끝에서와 같이 만들면 됩니다.

Combined two hand tips

middle finger, keeping the other fingers just as the scissors hand tips did.

This form uses Combined Two Hand Tips for attack and Combined(all) Two Hand Tips exerting stronger power than the single hand tip.

5.8 Combined(Joint) Three Hand Tips

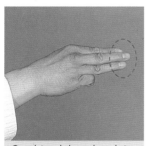

Combined three hand tips

Master   First, gather the first(index) finger and ring finger, laying the middle finger on them.

Next keep the remaining two fingers attached together loosely, then Combined Three Hand Tips are formed.

Those combined fingers form a triangle shape and three finger tips are used.

This is a variation of the Flat Hand Tips, exerting stronger power than the latter.

5.9 Combined(Joint) All Hand Tips

5.9-5.11

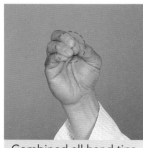

Combined all hand tips

Master   To form the Combined All Hand Tips, gather all five finger tips by sticking together, then bend the first joints of all fingers inward a little except the thumb.

이 모양은 모은 두 손끝을 공격에 사용하며, 한손끝보다 모은두손끝이 더 큰 힘을 가할 수 있습니다.

Words

scissor 가위
exert 가하다
remain 남다
triangle 삼각형
variation 변형

5.8 모은세손끝

사범 우선 집게손가락과 반지손가락(약지)을 모으고 가운데손가락을 두 손가락 사이에 놓으세요.

그리고 나머지 두 손가락을 같이 가볍게 붙이면 모은세손끝이 됩니다.

Expressions

attach together 함께
   붙이다
form a triangle shape
   삼각형 모양을 이루
   다
exert stronger power
   than ~ ~보다 강한
   힘을 가하다

모은세손끝은 삼각형 모양을 이루며, 세손끝이 사용됩니다.

이것은 편손끝의 변형인데, 편손끝보다 더 강한 힘을 가할 수 있습니다.

5.9 모둠손끝

사범 모둠손끝은 다섯손가락 끝을 모두 붙여 모으고, 엄지손가락을 제외한 모든 손가락의 첫 번째 마디를 안쪽으로 약간 굽히면 됩니다.

All combined five finger tips are applicable and used for the chopping technique at a shorter distance.

5.10 Bear Hand

Bear hand

Master   Bear Hand is formed almost the same way as the Flat Fist is formed.

The only difference is that all fingers except the thumb are bent harder than the flat fist.

Bear Hand uses the third joints of all fingers.

This is mainly applied for the hit technique, just hitting on the face.

At this moment, a hit is made inward just as a bear scratches with its fore foot sole.

5.11 Palm Hand

Palm hand

Master   Palm Hand is made by pulling the hand slightly upward in the direction of the hand back.

Then, bend the fingers lightly without any tension.

모은 다섯손끝 모두가 사용 가능하며, 짧은 거리에서 찍기 기술에 사용됩니다.

5.10 곰손

사범   곰손은 편주먹과 거의 비슷한 방식으로 만들어집니다.

한 가지 차이점은 엄지손가락을 제외한 모든 손가락이 편주먹에서보다 더 강하게 굽혀져 있다는 것입니다.

곰손은 모든 손가락의 마지막 세 번째 마디를 사용합니다.

곰손은 주로 치기 기술, 즉 얼굴을 칠 때 사용됩니다.

이때 치기는 안쪽으로 하는데, 곰이 앞발축으로 상처를 입히려는 것과 거의 같습니다.

5.11 바탕손

사범   바탕손은 손을 손등쪽으로 살짝 위로 올려 만듭니다.

그리고 손가락에 힘을 주지 말고 가볍게 굽혀주면 됩니다.

Words

chop 찍다
scratch 상처를 입히다
fore foot sole 앞발바
   닥, 앞발축
pull 당기다
tenseness 긴장

Expressions

at a shorter distance
짧은 거리에서
the same way 같은
   방법
in the direction of ~
   ~의 방향으로
without any tenseness
   힘을 주지 않고, 긴
   장하지 않고

At Palm Hand, the base of the palm is used, especially towards the wrist.

This is used for Hit and Defense techniques.

Meanwhile, it is so wide that it can not deliver vital parts; therefore, it is sometimes used for the defense technique.

5.12-5.13 5.12 Bent Wrist

Master   Bent Wrist is the opposite way of forming a Palm Hand.

The wrist is bowed fairly deep in the direction of the palm and five fingers are lightly gathered together.

The applicable part is the wrist on the side of bowed Hand Back.

Bent Wrist is used largely for the upward hit or the defense technique.

Unlike the palm hand which reaches long to make the punch technique, Bent Wrist can be applied to a fairly short distance attack because of the bent elbow.

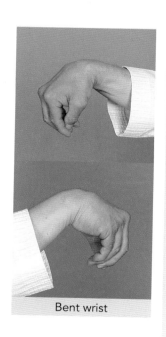

Bent wrist

바탕손에서는 손바닥의 밑, 구체적으로 팔목쪽을 사용하게 됩니다

바탕손은 치기와 막기 기술에 사용됩니다.

그런데 바탕손은 넓어서 중요 부위에 힘을 싣기 어렵습니다. 그래서 때때로 막기 기술에 사용되는 것입니다.

Words

Meanwhile 그런데
deliver 가지고 가다,
데려가다
opposite way 반대방식
bow 굽히다, 절하다

5.12 굽힌팔목

사범   굽힌팔목은 바탕손을 만들 때와 반대 방식입니다.

Expressions

unlike~ ~와는 다르게

팔목이 손바닥쪽으로 꽤 깊숙이 굽어지게 되며, 다섯손가락이 가볍게 같이 모이게 됩니다.

사용하는 부위는 굽혀진 손등의 측면에 있는 팔목입니다.

굽힌팔목은 대개 올려치기나 막기 기술에 사용됩니다.

지르기 기술을 하기 위해 길게 뻗는 바탕손과는 다르게, 굽힌팔목은 굽혀진 팔꿈치(팔굽) 때문에 아주 가까운 거리를 공격하기 위해 사용 됩니다.

Arc hand

5.13 Arc Hand

Master   To make Arc Hand, first keep the thumb and the first(index) finger wider and then open apart from each other.

Next, attach the four fingers except the thumb side by side, slightly bending each joint of the fingers so as to form a round shape.

The forearm and the Hand Back must be kept in a straight line so that it should not look like a Palm Hand.

Arc Hand uses the hollow part between the first (index) finger and the thumb and is usually used for the hit technique.

The jaw or neck are the best targets for the arc hand because they can fit the hollow of the arc hand.

If one hits the lower part of the jaw with the Arc Hand, the motion of executing such a technique is called Arc Hand Face Front Hit(or 'khaljaebi').

5.13 아금손

사범   아금손을 만들기 위해서는 먼저 엄지손가락과 집게손가락을 서로 떨어지게 하여 넓게 벌립니다.

다음으로, 둥근 형태를 만들기 위해 손가락들의 각 마디를 약간 굽히고, 엄지손가락을 제외한 네 손가락을 서로 붙입니다.

팔뚝과 손등은 바탕손처럼 보이지 않기 위해 일직선상에 있도록 합니다.

아금손은 집게손가락과 엄지손가락 사이의 빈 공간을 사용하며, 주로 치기 기술에 쓰입니다.

턱이나 목은 아금손의 파인 부분과 들어맞기 때문에 가장 좋은 목표물이 될 수 있습니다.

만약 아금손으로 턱의 아래 부위를 친다면, 그러한 기술을 사용하는 동작을 (얼굴)아금손앞치기(또는 칼재비)라고 부릅니다.

Words

fairly 꽤, 상당히
attach 붙이다
slightly 약간, 조금
hollow 파인, 쑥 들어
  간, 비어 있는
execute (기술을) 사용
  하다

Expressions

apart from ~로부터
  떨어지다
side by side 나란히
keep in a straight line
  일직선을 유지하다

6. Wrist

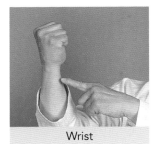

Wrist

Master   The Wrist is the part lying between the hand and the arm.

Inside, there are lots of muscles which move the hand and the wrist.

Wrist joints are related with diverse exercises such as bending, stretching, and leaning.

7. Forearm

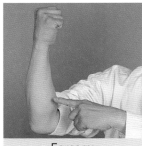

Forearm

Master   The forearm refers to the lower part of the arm, existing between the wrist and the elbow.

It has a big and long bone, which makes it easy to apply the defense technique.

Especially, the inner flank and the outer flank of the forearm are sharp enough to attack immediately after defending with either of them.

However, the forearm base and the forearm back are wide so they may be used in the defense technique.

6. 팔목

사범   팔목은 손과 팔 사이에 있는 부위입니다.

팔목에는 손가락과 팔목을 움직이는 많은 근육이 존재합니다.

그리고 팔목관절은 굽힘, 폄, 치우침 등 다양한 운동과 관련됩니다.

7. 팔뚝

사범   팔뚝은 팔목과 팔꿈치(팔굽) 사이에 있으며, 팔의 아래쪽 부위를 말합니다.

팔뚝에는 크고 긴 뼈가 있어 막기 기술에 쉽게 사용할 수 있습니다.

특히 팔뚝의 안과 바깥부위는 날카로워서 안 또는 바깥부위 중 하나로 방어를 하자마자 공격하기 좋습니다.

그러나 팔뚝의 등부위는 넓어서 막기 기술에 사용하는 것이 좋습니다.

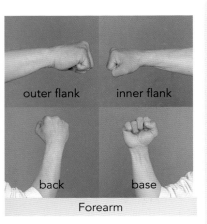

outer flank   inner flank

back   base

Forearm

Further, both the forearm base and forearm back are unable to inflict an attacking(offensive) blow, not being liable to suffer a fracture of bone if they are hit too hard.

The applicable parts of the forearm are outer flank of forearm, inner flank of forearm, back of forearm and base of forearm.

8. Elbow

Elbow

Wrist hitting

Master Elbow is the part in the middle of the arm where it bends, but its area is unclear.

When inflected at the joint in the middle of the arm, the elbow can be used to hit a near opponent.

At this moment, techniques such as spiral(turning) hit, lifting hit, downward hit, side hit and backward hit can be applied.

더군다나 팔뚝밑과 팔뚝등으로는 공격을 할 수 없고, 오히려 가격을 당하면 뼈가 부러져 고통을 겪을 수 있습니다.

팔뚝에서 사용 가능한 부위들은 바깥팔목, 안팔목, 등팔목과 밑팔목입니다.

8. 팔꿈치(팔굽)

사범 팔꿈치(팔굽)는 팔의 가운데에 접혀진 부위인데, 그 범위는 명확하지 않습니다.

팔 가운데 관절이 접혀진 상태의 팔꿈치(팔굽)는 가까이에 있는 상대방을 칠 때에 사용됩니다.

이때 돌려치기, 올려치기, 내려치기, 옆치기, 뒤치기 등의 기술이 적용될 수 있습니다.

9-9.3

9. Foot

Leg and foot

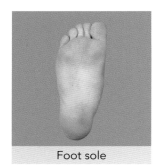

Foot sole

Master   Two legs and feet enable us to keep the balance of the body in standing, moving, turning, lowering and lifting, high and broad jumping, kicking, defending, etc.

Also, the various parts of the foot sole can be used in many ways as sharp weapons in kicking technique.

Foot techniques are not like the hand or fist techniques in terms of speed, flexibility and accuracy, which naturally requires more training.

When one applies a foot technique, the body has the difficulty to keep itself stabilized on one foot, thus resulting in falling or failing in attack.

Not to meet this situation and to get speedier and better foot techniques, one requires a long and hard training.

The merits of foot techniques are their stronger power than any other techniques and their capability of delivering attack at a distance.

9. 발

사범 두 다리와 발은 우리가 서 있고, 움직이고, 돌고, 낮추고, 높이고, 높게 그리고 넓게 뛰고, 차고, 막을 때 몸의 균형을 잡아줍니다.

또한 발바닥의 여러 부분들은 주로 차기 기술에서 날카로운 무기로 다양하게 사용될 수 있습니다.

발을 사용하는 기술은 근본적으로 많은 훈련을 필요로 하며, 또 속도, 유연성과 정확성 면에서 손 또는 주먹 기술과 다릅니다.

발기술을 사용할 때에는 한쪽 발로 몸의 균형을 유지하는 것이 어렵습니다. 따라서 넘어지기 쉽고 공격에 실패하기 쉽습니다.

이러한 경우를 당하지 않고 더 빠르고 좋은 발기술을 구사하려면 오랜 기간에 걸친 힘든 훈련을 해야 합니다.

발기술의 장점은 다른 어떤 기술보다 강한 힘에 있으며, 먼 거리를 공격할 수 있는 점을 들 수 있습니다.

Words

foot sole 발바닥
sharp 날카로운
flexibility 유연성
accuracy 정확성
stabilize 안정시키다
capability 능력, 역량

Expressions

in many ways 다양한 방법으로
in terms of ~의 측면에서
at a distance 먼 거리에서

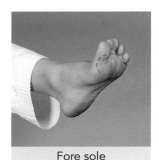

Fore sole

9.1 Fore Sole

Master   Fore Sole is the most important part of the sole and the base of tiptoes when tiptoes are bent upward.

When the body turns, the Fore Sole plays the role of an axis.

The Fore Sole is used in Front Kick, Spiral(Turning) Kick, Twist Kick, and Dichotomy(Semilunar) Kick techniques, and so forth.

It also plays the role of a brake as the body moves.

9.2 Back Sole

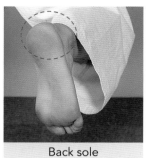

Back sole

Master   The Back Sole is the hidden part of the sole.

This also applies itself in pounding, Side Kick and Stretched Kick techniques.

9.3 Tiptoe

Master   Tiptoe is the end part of toes when they are stretched straight forward.

9.1 앞축(앞발바닥)

사범 앞축은 축의 가장 중요한 부위이며, 발끝이 위로 굽혀져 있을 때 발끝을 지탱해주는 부위가 됩니다.

몸이 회전할 때 앞축은 중심축 역할을 합니다.

앞축은 앞차기, 돌려차기, 비틀어차기, 반달차기 등의 기술에 사용됩니다.

앞축은 몸이 이동할 때 제동 역할도 한다.

9.2 뒤축(뒤발바닥)

사범 뒤축은 축에서 보이지 않는 부위를 말합니다.

뒤축도 역시 찔기, 옆차기, 뻗어차기 기술에 사용됩니다.

9.3 발끝

사범 발끝은 발가락이 직선으로 뻗어 있을 때 끝부위를 말합니다.

Words

fore sole 앞축(앞발바닥)
important 중요안
tiptoe 발끝
axis 축
dichotomy 양분, 이분
semilunar 반달
brake 제동
back sole 뒤축(뒤발바닥)
pounding 찔기

Expressions

plays the role of~ ~의 역할을 하다
and so forth ~등
the hidden part 숨겨진 부분
the end part 끝 부분

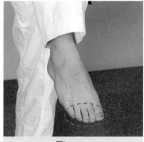

Tiptoe

Stretch kick

Foot blade

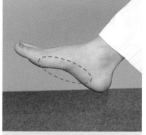

Foot blade back

Tiptoe is applied to the Stretch(Stretched) Kick with the spring power of the leg swinging from the knee.

It is used in the Front Kick and the Twist Kick.

This kick principally aims at the opponent's groin or at the solar plexus, if one becomes more skilled.

This technique is performed with the first toe directed upward like the case of the thumb at Erected(Vertical) Hand Tips Thrusting.

 9.4 Foot Blade

Master Foot Blade refers to the outer side between the sole and the foot back, ranging from the outer rim of the heel to the last toe.

It is used in Side Kick, defense (or kick up) and counter kick techniques.

9.5 Foot Blade Back, Back of the Foot Blade

Master Foot Blade Back is the opposite side of foot blade (the inner side of the foot), ranging from the inner heel to the inner side of the fore sole.

발끝은 무릎부위부터 휙 움직여서 발로 튕기는 힘으로 차는 뻗어차기에 사용됩니다.

이것은 앞차기와 비틀어차기에 사용됩니다.

이 기술을 좀 더 숙달해서 사용할 수 있다면 주로 상대방의 낭심이나 명치를 목표로 할 수 있습니다.

이 기술은 세운손끝찌르기와 같이 발을 안으로 틀어 엄지발가락을 위로 한 채 찹니다.

9.4 발날

사범   발날은 축(발바닥)과 발등 사이의 바깥쪽에 있는 옆면을 말하며, 뒤꿈치의 가장자리부터 마지막 발가락에 해당하는 부위입니다.

옆차기, 막기(또는 차올리기), 받아차기 거술에 쓰입니다.

9.5 발날등

사범   발날등은 발날의 반대쪽(발의 안쪽 옆면)을 말하며, 안쪽뒤꿈치부터 앞축의 안쪽면까지 해당합니다.

Words

principally 주로
groin 사타구니(서혜부), 낭심
rim 가장자리
counter kick 받아차기
opposite side 반대쪽

Expressions

applied to~ ~에 사용되다
aim at~ ~를 목표로 하다
performed with ~ ~를 가지고 수행하다
range from~ ~에 걸쳐있다.

This part is wide so it is used in defense and kick techniques, and mainly in Target Kick.

9.6 Heel

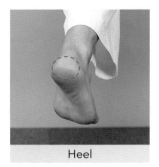

Heel

Master   Heel refers to the lower part of the foot heel.

This is used in Downward(Drop) Kick, Body Spiral(Turning) Thrashing Kick, and Hooking Kick techniques.

9.7 Sole

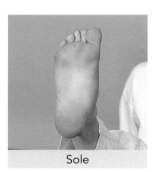

Sole

Master   The Sole-related part covers from the Back Sole to the toes including the Fore Sole.

This is used in Body Spiral(Turning) Thrashing Kick and Downward(Drop) Kick techniques.

9.8 Top of the Foot

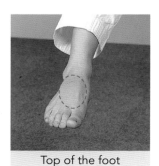

Top of the foot

Master   The Top of the foot is the upper part of the foot, ranging from the ankle to the toes.

When applied to technique, the ankle needs to be stretched.

이 부위는 넓어서 막기와 차기 기술에 사용되며, 주로 표적차기에 사용됩니다.

9.6 뒤꿈치

사범 뒤꿈치는 발뒤꿈치의 아래 부위를 말합니다.

뒤꿈치는 내려차기, 몸돌려후려차기, 낚아차기 기술에 사용됩니다.

9.7 발바닥

사범 발바닥에 해당하는 부위는 뒤축부터 앞축을 포함한 발가락까지를 말합니다.

발바닥은 몸돌려후려차기와 내려차기 기술에 사용됩니다.

9.8 발등

사범 발등은 발목부터 발가락까지에 걸친 발의 위쪽 부위입니다.

발등을 사용할 때는 발목을 펴야 합니다.

Words

mainly 주로
sole-related 발바닥과 관련된
include 포함하다
ankle 발목

Expressions

cover from~ ~에 걸쳐있다
needs to 필요하다, 해야한다.

This is used in Upward Kick, Spiral(Turning) Kick and Thrash Kick techniques.

10. Shin

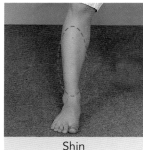

Shin

Master The shin refers to the part to which the front bone of the lower leg belongs and ranges from the ankle to the knee joint in the front.

The shin is mainly used at the defense technique, but is also vulnerable to the opponent's attack.

For this reason, one feels pain when the shin collides with the opponent's kick.

11. Knee

Knee

Master The knee refers to the knee joint and its surrounding parts.

If the knee is inflected, it is solid enough to hit the opponent strongly, especially effective for the lift up hit technique.

발등은 올려차기, 돌려차기, 후려차기 기술에 사용됩니다.

10. 정강이

사범 정강이는 아랫다리의 앞쪽 뼈가 있는 부분이며, 앞쪽의 발목부터 무릎관절에 이릅니다.

정강이는 주로 막기 기술에 사용되는데, 상대방의 공격에 쉽게 다칠 수 있습니다.

이런 이유로 정강이가 상대방의 차기에 맞으면 고통스러울 수 있습니다.

11. 무릎

사범 무릎은 무릎관절과 그 주변부를 포함하는 신체부위를 말합니다.

만약 무릎이 접혀져 있다면 단단해져서 상대방을 강하게 찰 때 사용할 수 있으며, 특히 올려치기와 돌려치기 기술에 효과적입니다.

Lift up hit

Master   Up to now, we've learned about eleven body parts.
Thank you for your effort.

Disciple Thank you for your effort as well, master.

사범	이상으로 열한 가지 신체부위에 대해 알아보았습니다. 모두 수고하셨습니다.
문하생	네, 감사합니다. 사범님도 수고하셨습니다.

Expressions

up to now 지금까지, 이상으로
learn about~ ~를 배우다
as well 또한

Part 2
Basic Movements of Taekwondo

태권도의 기본 동작

Master   From now, we will exercise basic movements of Taekwondo one by one.

You are requested to learn these basic movements thoroughly to easily proceed to the next steps for specific techniques.

Any questions? Please do not hesitate to ask .

Disciple   I have one. What kind of basic movements should we learn? How long will it take for us to exercise all those things?

Blocking

Master   Good questions. Mainly, we will focus on six basic movements such as stance, blocking, punch(ing), hit(ing), thrusting, and kick(ing). Next, we could add some more important ones including grasping, breaking, throwing down, and Special Poom.

Disciple   It seems like it would take quite a long period of training.

Master   When it comes to the period, well, you must exercise continuously for the actual fight. Further, intensive and repetitive training over more than a year should be backed up.

사범 오늘 수업부터는 기본동작을 하나씩 연습하겠습니다.

기본이 잘 갖추어져야 세부 기술을 제대로 수행할 수 있으므로 완벽하게 익히기 바랍니다.

질문 있나요? 궁금한 것 있으면 무엇이든 물어 보세요.

문하생 네, 어떤 기본동작들을 배우게 되는 건가요? 모두 익히는 데 어느 정도 걸리는가요?

사범 좋은 질문입니다. 먼저 서기, 막기, 지르기, 치기, 찌르기, 그리고 차기의 여섯 가지 기본동작에 중점을 둘 것입니다. 다음으로 잡기, 꺾기, 넘기기, 특수품을 포함한 몇 가지 중요한 것들을 추가할 수 있습니다.

문하생 상당한 기간의 수련이 필요할 것 같은데요?

사범 기간에 대해서는 글쎄요. 모든 동작을 실전에 제대로 활용할 수 있도록 익히려면 꾸준한 연습이 필요하겠고요. 최소한 1년 이상 반복적이고 강도 높은 훈련이 뒷받침되어야할 것입니다.

Words

exercise 연습, 훈련
thoroughly 완벽하게, 철저히
specific 세부적인
hesitate 망설이다
continuously 꾸준하게
actual fight 실전
intensive 강도높은
repetitive 반복적인

Expressions

from now 지금부터
one by one 하나씩
be requested to~ ~해야 한다.
focus on~ _에 중점을 두다

Disciple It seems like a strenuous season to us. We are nervous.

Master Don't be worried and just follow me, guys. You must strive for your dreams. Let's get started!

1. Stance

Master The first basic movement is 'Stance'.

Stance

The stance means keeping any part of the body except the two feet not touching the ground or the floor, using the lower part of the body.

The upper part of the body including the arms can make free motions, but the trunk should be kept always erect.

The stance techniques give great influence over the movement of the center of gravity and the center of weight, and there are various stance techniques according to the positions and movements of the two legs.

Sometimes a ponderous posture makes the stance technique ready for defense, and at times an

문하생 힘든 한 해가 되겠군요. 긴장되네요.

사범 걱정하지 말고 저를 따라오세요. 여러분, 꿈을 이루기 위해서는 노력해야겠죠. 자, 그럼 시작해 봅시다!

1. 서기

사범 첫 번째로 배울 동작은 '서기'입니다.

서기는 하체를 이용하여 두 발을 제외한 몸의 어떤 부위라도 바닥에 닿지 않도록 하는 것입니다.

팔을 포함하여 상체는 자유롭게 움직일 수 있으니 몸통은 항상 똑바로 세운 채로 있어야 합니다.

서기 기술은 중력과 무게중심의 이동에 큰 영향을 미치며, 두 다리의 위치와 움직임에 따라 다양한 서기 기술들이 있습니다.

때로는 육중한 자세가 서기 기술로 방어를 잘 할 수 있게 하고, 다른 경우에는 불안정한 서기가 중심 이동을 빠르게 하며 강한 힘을 행사

Words

strenuous 힘든
nervous 신경쓰이는, 긴장된
except ~를 제외하고
erect 세우다
center of gravity 무게중심
ponderous 육중한, 묵직한
posture 자세

Expressions

strive for~ ~를 위한 노력하다
get started 시작하다
give influences 영향을 주다
according to~ ~에 따라

unstabilized stance makes the movement of the center speedy and exerts impulsive forces so that one may be ready to take next actions swiftly.

The types of stance are classified according to the position of feet, either widened apart side by side or fore and back and according to the way of keeping the knee, either stretched or inflected.

1.1 Open Stance

1.1.1 Parallel Stance

Parallel stance

Master   The breadth of the two feet will be one foot wide, the inner sides foot blade back of both feet paralleling with each other, both knees are stretched.

And both legs will support your weight evenly, the center of balance coming between the legs.

This is a fundamental pattern of stance to be used in the standstill posture or as a 'ready stance'.

1.1.2 Right Side Stance

Right side stance

Master   First, take the same pose as the parallel stance, and then move only the fore sole of the right foot

하게 하여 다음 동작을 신속하게 할 수 있게 해줍니다.

서기의 유형은 양 발의 위치가 서로 넓게 또는 앞뒤로 벌려져 있거나, 무릎을 뻗거나 굽히게 하는 방식에 따라 분류합니다.

Words

unstabilized 불안정한
impulsive 충동적인
swiftly 신속히
fundamental 기본적인
standstill 정지, 멈춤

1.1. 넓혀서기

1.1.1 나란히서기

사범 두 발의 간격은 한 발 너비 정도이며, 양 발의 발날등 안쪽은 서로 평행이 되게 하며, 양 무릎은 곧게 뻗습니다.

Expressions

side by side 좌우로
fore and back 앞뒤로
paralleling with~ ~와
  평행하다

그리고 양 다리는 체중을 균형 있게 지탱해 주어야 하며, 균형의 중심은 양 다리 사이에 있게 됩니다.

이 자세는 정지 자세 또는 준비 서기에서 사용되는 기본적인 서기입니다.

1.1.2 오른서기

사범 먼저 나란히서기 자세를 취한 후 뒤꿈치로 중심을 잡으며, 오른발의 앞축을 90도 오른쪽으로 옮깁니다.

90 degrees rightwards, pivoting on the heel.

This is used in Hammer Fist Downward Hit and Back Fist Outward Hit techniques.

🎧 `1.1.3-1.1.7` 1.1.3 Left Side Stance

Left side stance

Master Every movement is quite the opposite way of Right Side Stance.

Namely, take the same pose as the parallel stance, and then move only the fore sole of the left foot 90 degrees leftward, pivoting on the heel.

The usage is also the same as the Right Side Stance.

1.1.4 At Ease Stance

At ease stance

Master Keep the breadth of two heels at one foot's length, each fore sole opened outward by 60 degrees, the knees straightened, and make the two legs support the body weight evenly, slightly leaning on the back sole side.

This stance is generally used for a ready stance.

이 기술은 메주먹내려치기와 등주먹바깥치기에서 사용됩니다.

1.1.3 왼서기

사범 모든 동작이 오른서기의 반대입니다.

즉, 나란히서기 자세를 취한 후 뒤꿈치로 중심을 잡고, 왼발의 앞축을 90도 왼쪽으로 옮깁니다.

쓰임새도 역시 오른서기와 같습니다.

1.1.4 편히서기

사범 두 뒤꿈치 사이의 간격을 한 발 길이로 하고, 각각의 앞축을 밖으로 60도 되도록 오픈하고, 무릎은 똑바로 펴고 약간 뒤축쪽에 기대듯이 하여 두 다리가 무게를 균형 있게 지탱하게 합니다.

이 자세는 일반적으로 준비자세에서 사용됩니다.

Words

pivot 회전하다, 회전
  시키다
opposite way 반대의
  방법
usage 쓰임새
straighten 펴다
generally 일반적으로

Expressions

used in~ ~에 사용되다
leaning on 기대다

1.1.5 Inward Stance

Inward stance

Master   Keep the breadth of two fore soles at one foot length, each back sole opened outward by 60 degrees.

Also keep the knees straightened and make the two legs support the body weight evenly, slightly leaning on the fore sole side.

The pose is the opposite way of At Ease Stance.

This stance is generally used for a ready stance, aimed at developing the strength of the legs.

1.1.6 Riding Stance

Riding stance

Master   This stance makes the width between both legs two feet length with its legs slightly bent.

When the knees of both legs looked down, the knees are slightly bent and on a straight line with tiptoes.

The trunk stands upright and two knees and shins are also erected.

1.1.5 안쫑서기

사범 두 발의 앞축 사이의 간격은 '한 발' 길이로 하고, 각각의 뒤축은 바깥으로 60도 벌려줍니다.

또한 두 무릎은 펴고 두 다리로 체중을 지탱하며, 앞축이 있는 쪽으로 약간 기울입니다.

이 자세는 편히서기의 반대 방식입니다.

이 자세는 일반적으로 준비자세에서 사용되며, 다리의 힘을 키우기 위해 고안된 것입니다.

1.1.6 주춤서기

사범 이 서기는 두 다리 사이의 간격은 두 발 길이 정도로 하고, 다리를 약간 굽히고 있는 자세입니다.

두 다리의 무릎은 내려봤을 때 무릎과 발끝이 일치되도록 굽혀 서게 됩니다.

몸통은 반듯하게 하고, 두 무릎과 정강이를 반듯하게 세웁니다.

Words

breadth 너비
upright (자세가) 바른, 꼿꼿한
fore sole 앞축

Expressions

one foot length 한 발 길이
opened outward 바깥으로 벌리다
keep straightened 편 상태를 유지하다
aim at~ ~를 목표로 하다

1.1.7 Lowered Riding Stance

Master This is proceeded with the same way as the riding stance except that the legs should be open wider, keeping the body lower.

The low center of weight makes the body the most balanced, but it needs more strength in making every action due to less impulsive force.

Therefore, this is generally used for developing the power.

▶ 1.1.8-1.1.11 1.1.8 Oblique Angle Stance

Master In a parallel stance, just put one foot (left or right) straight forward one step.

The body weight should be supported by both legs evenly, the center or balance coming from the legs.

When the left foot is put forward, it is called a Left Side Oblique Angle Stance, and the opposite way a Right Side Oblique Angle Stance.

Oblique angle stance

1.1.7 낮추어서기

사범 이것은 주춤서기와 같은 방식인데요. 두 발을 조금 더 넓게 벌리고 몸을 더 낮추어 서는 점이 다릅니다.

중심이 낮으므로 몸을 가장 안정감 있게 만듭니다. 그러나 순발력이 줄어들어 모든 동작을 할 때 힘이 더 들어가게 됩니다.

따라서 이것은 일반적으로 힘을 키우기 위해 사용됩니다.

1.1.8 모서기

사범 나란히서기에서 어느 한 발(왼발 또는 오른발)을 '한 발' 길이로 앞으로 내딛는 것입니다.

체중이 두 다리에 똑같이 실려야 하며, 중심 또는 균형은 두 다리 사이에 있습니다.

만약 왼발을 앞으로 내딛으면 왼모서기, 반대의 경우는 오른모서기라 합니다.

Words

impulsive 충동적인
develope 증진시키다
balance 균형

Expressions

proceeded with~ ~를
  계속하다
open wider 더 넓게
  벌리다
due to~ ~ 때문에

Oblique angle riding stance

Inward riding stance

Forward stance

1.1.9 Oblique Angle Riding Stance

Master In a Riding Stance, the right or left foot only will be put straight forward one step.

This is used in attack(offense) and defense, moving aside during the opponent's attacks.

1.1.10 Inward Riding Stance

Master Also in a riding stance, only the fore soles of both feet will look inward pulling the back soles outward.

This usage is the same as a riding stance, using to strengthen the power of the lower muscle.

1.1.11 Forward Stance

Master This is just like the stance when one stops walking with a forward step.

The distance of the two feet is one step long, the inner sides of two feet must be on a straight line,

The two knees should be kept straightened, the weight being supported by both legs evenly.

1.1.9 모주춤서기

사범 이것은 주춤서기에서 오른발 또는 왼발 한 쪽만을 한 발 길이만큼 앞으로 곧게 내딛으면 됩니다.

이것은 공격과 방어에 사용되며, 상대방의 공격 중에 옆으로 피해 움직입니다.

1.1.10 안쫑주춤서기

사범 이것은 주춤서기에서 뒤축은 바깥쪽으로 당기고, 두 발의 앞축만이 안쪽으로 향하게 합니다.

이 사용법은 주춤서기와 같은데요, 아래(하체) 근육의 힘을 더 강하게 하기 위함입니다.

1.1.11 앞서기

사범 걷다가 멈추었을 때와 같이 서는 것입니다.

두 발 사이의 간격은 한 걸음의 길이이고, 두 발 사이의 안쪽은 일직선에 놓여야 합니다.

두 무릎은 뻗어져 있어야 하며, 체중은 두 다리로 균형 있게 지탱됩니다.

It is permitted to keep the hind foot slightly turned from the straight line within the angle of 30 degrees in order to allow a natural pose.

Generally, this is for the attacking(offensive) purpose, but sometimes for the defensive purpose, too.

▶ 1.1.12-1.1.14 1.1.12 Forward Riding Stance

Forward riding stance

Master This is the same as the front stance except that the knees are lowered like the riding stance.

In taking this pose, the back sole of the fore foot is likely to be pushed outward, but the angle of turning should be kept within 30 degrees.

The weight should be supported by both feet, raising the back soles slightly so that impulsive force can be exerted.

This is used in the posture of aiming at the target during Kyorugi and can make very impulsive motions.

뒷발은 다음 자세를 자연스럽게 취하기 위해 일직선이 아닌 30도 정도로 벌립니다.

일반적으로 공격을 위해 사용되지만, 때때로 방어 목적으로도 쓰입니다.

1.1.12 앞주춤서기

사범 이것은 앞서기와 같으나, 주춤서기와 같이 두 무릎이 낮추어지는 것이 다릅니다.

이 자세를 취할 때에는 앞에 있는 발의 뒤축이 밖으로 물러나듯이 하며, (몸을) 회전하는 각도가 30도가 넘지 않도록 합니다.

체중은 두 다리에 똑같이 실려야 하며, 순발력을 발휘하기 위해 뒤축을 살짝 들어올립니다.

이것은 겨루기에서 목표물을 조준하기 위한 자세로 쓰이며, 매우 순발력이 있습니다.

Words

slightly 약간
natural 자연스러운
lower 낮추다

Expressions

in order to~ ~하기 위하여
likely to ~해야 할 듯 하다
aim at ~를 목표로 하다

1.1.13 Forward Inflection Stance

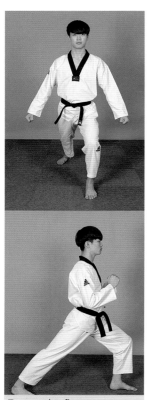

Forward inflection stance

Master The vertical distance between the two feet is one and a half steps.

And the parallel distance between the two feet is one fist.

The tiptoes of the front foot place forward, lower the knee in order to match your knee and tiptoes when you look down in an upright standing position.

Keep the back sole turned inward within the angle of 30 degrees and stretch the knee of the hind leg and put the balance of your weight forward by two-thirds.

Stand upright and twist your body forward at an angle of 30 degrees.

This stance makes it easy to push forward, thereby enabling one to perform attack techniques.

1.1.14 Backward Inflection Stance

Master Let me explain it in case of Righthand Backward Inflection Stance.

1.1.13 앞굽이

사범   두 발 사이의 간격은 한 걸음 반입니다.

그리고 두 발 안쪽 사이의 평행 간격은 한 주먹 정도입니다.

앞발의 끝을 앞으로 내딛으며, 위로 곧바로 선 자세에서 아래로 볼 때 무릎과 발끝이 일치하도록 무릎을 낮춥니다.

뒤축이 30도 이내로 안으로 굽히고 뒤에 있는 발의 무릎을 뻗고 체중의 3분의 2 정도는 앞쪽에 둡니다.

몸을 위로 바로 세우고 30도 각도로 몸을 앞으로 비틀어줍니다.

이 서기는 앞으로 밀기를 쉽게 해주며, 이로 인해 공격 기술을 잘 수행하도록 만들어줍니다.

1.1.14 뒷굽이

사범   오른뒷굽이의 경우로 설명해보겠습니다.

Words

vertical 수직의, 세로의
half step 반 걸음
match 일치하다
explain 설명하다

Expressions

turn inward 안으로 굽히다
by two-thirds 2/3 정도
Stand upright 위로 세우다
makes it easy 쉽게하다
in case of ~의 경우

Backward inflection stance

From the Close Stance, the fore sole or right foot is opened at an angle of 90 degrees, pivoting on the back sole,

Then the left foot is put two steps forward from the heel of the right foot, making an angle of 90 degrees and the body is lowered by the inflection of two knees.

The inflection of the right foot knee will keep an angle of 60 to 70 degrees between the ground and the shin.

And the inflection of the left foot knee will be an angle of 100 to 110 degrees between the ground and the left shin.

The two knees inwardly like the Forward Riding Stance, and the center of weight as well as the center of balance will be laid on the right foot by two thirds.

1.1.15 Inverted '⊤' Shape Stance

Master This stance is almost the same as the Backward Inflection Stance, except that the forward foot makes a right square with the back foot.

모아서기에서 앞축 또는 오른발 뒤축을 중심점으로 해서 90도 각도로 벌려줍니다.

그리고 왼발은 오른발 뒤꿈치에서 두 발 앞으로 내딛어 90도 각도를 이루며, 두 무릎을 굽혀서 몸을 낮춥니다.

Words

inflection 굽이, 굽힘
ground 바닥
shin 정강이
Invert 뒤집다

오른쪽 무릎의 굽이는 바닥과 정강이 사이의 각도로 60 내지 70도로 유지합니다.

그리고 왼쪽 무릎의 굽이는 바닥과 정강이 사이의 각도가 100 내지 110도 되게 합니다.

Expressions

as well as ~뿐 아니라
lay on ~위에 놓다

두 무릎은 안쪽으로 앞주춤서기와 같이 되며, 무게중심과 균형의 중심은 3분의 2 정도 오른발에 놓이게 됩니다.

1.1.15 ㄱ자서기

사범 이 자세는 뒷굽이와 거의 같으나, 앞에 내딛은 발이 뒤쪽 발에서 정면으로 나와 있습니다.

In other words, the extended line of the forward foot's sole crosses the center of Foot Blade's back of the back foot, thus the two soles forming an inverted 'T' letter shape.

This forward leg with an inside position is ready to defend one's groin from the opponent's attack and to deliver trunk spiral(turning) kick techniques.

This is a defensive posture as well as a surprise attack(offense) stance.

1.1.16 Tiger Stance

Master   When we first hear about tiger stance, we are reminded of atiger, aren't we? It's one type of stance but I do not know of the origin of the expression.

The following explanation is the case of Right Hand Tiger Stance.

From the position of a close stance, the left foot is put one foot forward.

And the right foot is opening the fore sole 30 degrees based on the back sole.

Tiger stance

바꾸어 말하면 앞으로 내딛은 다리 축의 연장선이 뒷발의 발날등 가운데로 교차되므로 두 발의 축이 'ㄴ'자와 같이 되는 것입니다.

이렇게 안쪽에 위치한 앞으로 내딛은 다리는 상대방의 공격으로부터 낭심을 방어하고, 또한 몸돌려차기를 하기 위해서입니다.

이것은 기습공격 자세이자 방어 자세입니다.

1.1.16 범서기

사범 '범서기'를 처음 들으면 바로 호랑이를 연상하게 되죠? 서기의 한 종류인데, 왜 호랑이를 빗대어 표현하게 된 것인지는 저도 잘 모르겠네요.

아래 설명은 오른범서기의 경우입니다.

모아서기 위치에서 왼발을 한 발 앞으로 내딛습니다.

그리고 뒤축에 중심을 두고 오른발의 앞축을 30도로 넓혀 섭니다.

Words

extended line 연장선
cross 교차하다
inverted 뒤집힌
remind 연상하다
origin 어원, 근원

Expressions

in other words 다시 말하면
defend one's groin 낭심을 보호하다
based on ~에 중심을 두다

The left foot in front will keep the ankle stretched so that its tiptoes or the fore sole alone may lightly touch the ground, and the knee will bend down as much as it is required.

Then concentrate the force on the lower abdomen, the weight is supported 100% by the right foot.

This stance is mainly used in attack(offense), applying counter kicks with the front foot, as it is not supporting the weight, and at times returning counterattack, or blocking the opponent's attack of the shin to counterattack with hands.

1.2-1.2.3 1.2 Close Stance

Master   Stand upright with both inner feet blades attached and stretch both knees.

This is used in Attention Stance, Overlapped Hands Ready Stance, Covered Fist Ready Stance, and Fists on the Waist Ready Stance.

1.2.1 Attention Stance

Attention stance

Master   From a Close Stance, the back soles are left attached to each other but only the fore soles are

앞에 있는 왼발의 발목을 펴고 발끝, 또는 앞축만으로 가볍게 바닥을 딛고 무릎을 필요한 만큼 아래로 굽혀줍니다.

그리고 나서 아랫배에 힘을 주며, 체중은 오른발에 100% 싣습니다.

주로 공격에 사용하며, 앞의 발에 체중이 실리지 않으므로 받아차기를 하고, 때로는 반격을 하며, 또는 상대방의 정강이 공격을 막고 두 손으로 역습하기도 합니다.

Words

stretch 펴다
concentrate 집중하다
abdomen 배
counterattack 받아차기
overlap 겹치다

Expressions

in front 앞에 있는
as much as ~한 만큼

1.2. 모아서기

사범 두 발날 안쪽을 서로 맞대고 서서 양쪽 무릎을 펴 줍니다.

이 기술은 차렷서기, 겹손준비서기, 보주먹준비서기, 두주먹허리자세에 이용됩니다.

1.2.1 뒤축모아서기

사범 모아서기에서 뒤축들이 서로 붙게 하고, 앞축만 각도를 60도로 넓혀서게 됩니다.

opened at an angle of 60 degrees.

It is used in applicable action of stance.

1.2.2 Reverse Attention Stance

Reverse attention stance

Master From a Close Stance, the first toes of the feet are attached to each other, opening the back soles apart from each other at an angle of 60 degrees.

This is the reverse stance of the Back Sole Close Stance.

Both the Fore Sole Close Stance and Back Sole Close Stance are used to ready stances in a state of halt.

1.2.3 Assisting Stance

Assisting stance

Master The front foot, at its foot blade back, is touched by the first toe of the assisting foot and the latter's back sole is lifted.

That is, only the fore sole touches the ground,

The body is lowered by bending the knees as in the Riding Stance.

서기의 응용 행동으로 사용됩니다.

1.2.2 앞축모아서기

사범 모아서기에서 발의 첫 번째(엄지)발가락이 서로 붙게 하고, 뒤축은 60도 각도로 넓혀줍니다.

이 서기는 뒤축모아서기의 반대입니다.

앞축모아서기와 뒤축모아서기는 멈춘 상태에서 준비서기로 사용됩니다.

1.2.3 곁다리서기

사범 앞발의 발날등에 다른 발의 첫 번째(엄지)발가락이 닿게 하며, 다른 발의 뒤축은 들어줍니다.

즉, 앞축만 바닥을 닿게 하는 것이죠.

몸은 주춤서기에서처럼 무릎을 굽혀서 낮춥니다.

Words
applicable 응용가능한
reverse 반대의
lift 들어올리다

Expressions
apart from~ ~로부터 떨어지다
in a state of halt 멈춘 상태에서

The weight is supported only by the front foot, the assisting foot merely helping keep the balance.

This stance is used to make one thrust forward like an onrush.

 1.2.4 Forward Cross Stance

Master In case of a Righthand Forward Cross Stance, the whole actions are as follows.

Forward cross stance

A Righthand Forward Cross Stance is a suspended stance of the momentary action when you move your right foot left bound from either a Riding Stance or Lowered Riding Stance.

Draw your right foot to cross over the back of the left foot and place its fore sole by the smallest toe of the left foot.

The movement should be made with the knees kept bent down and the shins of both feet will make an 'X' sign, crossing with each other, keeping the two feet as near as possible,

And when you pause in a Righthand Forward Cross Stance for a certain action, you must make

무게는 앞발에 의해서만 지탱되고, 다른 발은 균형을 유지하는 데 약간 도움을 주는 정도입니다.

이 자세는 급격하게 돌진하는 것처럼 앞으로 찌르기를 할 수 있게 합니다.

1.2.4 앞꼬아서기

사범 오른앞꼬아서기의 경우 전체 움직임은 다음과 같습니다.

오른앞꼬아서기는 주춤서기 또는 낮추어주춤서기에서 오른발을 왼쪽으로 옮길 때의 순간 동작이 중지된 자세입니다.

오른발을 끌어서 왼발의 등 위로 지나치고, 오른발의 앞축은 왼발의 새끼발가락옆에 놓습니다.

이 움직임은 무릎이 아래로 굽혀지고, 두 발의 정강이와 종아리를 붙여 서로 엇갈리게(X자 모양) 합니다.

어떤 동작을 하기 위해 오른앞꼬아서기로 멈추어 서면 오른발의 모든 축이 무게를 지탱하면서 바닥에 닿게 하고, 왼발의 앞축만 가지고 바

Words

merely 거의
onrush 돌격
momentary 순간의
draw 당기다

Expressions

in case of ~의 경우에
bend down 아래로 굽히다
as near as possible 최대한 가까이

the whole sole of the right foot touch the ground, supporting your weight, and keep the left foot touching the ground only at its fore sole.

This stance is mainly used to move sideways.

1.2.5 Backward Cross Stance

Backward cross stance

Master The right foot thrusts forward pounding the ground and at the same time the left foot follows, placing its toes near the right foot blade to brake the movement.

At this point, the right calf will stick to the left shin, making an 'x' sign, and the two knees are also bent down.

With this stance, you can pound on your opponent's foot back, approaching nearer for a second attack.

1.2.6 Crane Stance

Crane stance

Master This stance looks like when a crane lifts its one leg.

First, bend and lower your right knee as in the Riding Stance and then lift up your left foot so

닥에 닿도록 유지해야 합니다.

이 서기는 옆으로 움직일 때 주로 사용됩니다.

1.2.5 뒤꼬아서기

사범 오른발이 바닥을 찧으며 앞으로 지르듯이 나가고 동시에 왼발이 뒤 따르며, 발가락을 오른발등에 가깝게 두어 움직임에 제동을 걸어줍 니다.

이 순간에 오른쪽 장딴지는 왼쪽 정강이에 밀착하여 'X' 모양을 만들 며, 두 무릎도 같이 굽혀지게 합니다.

이 서기로서 상대의 발등을 찧으며 가깝게 접근하면서 2차 공격 시 에 사용합니다.

1.2.6 학다리서기

사범 이 서기는 학이 한쪽 다리를 들고 서 있는 모습과 같습니다.

먼저, 주춤서기에서와 같이 오른쪽 무릎을 굽혀 낮추고 왼발을 들어 올려 발날등이 오른쪽 무릎의 안쪽에 가깝도록 합니다.

Words

support 지탱하다, 지 지하다
mainly 주로
thrust 찌르다
pound 찧다
place 두다, 놓다
crane 학

Expressions

move sidewards 옆으 로 움직이다
brake the movement 동작에 제동을 걸다
stick to ~에 밀착하다
approach nearer 가깝 게 접근하다
look like~ ~처럼 보 이다

that the Foot Blade Back (back of foot blade) may be placed close to the inner side of the right knee.

In this stance, the lifted left knee will be tightened to protrude forward. If the left knee opens outward, keeping balance will be difficult, and the next motion for an attack will be dull.

This stance helps exercise the maintenance of balance and arouses confusion in the opponent because of your readiness to deliver kicks at any moment.

1.2.7 Reverse Crane Stance

Master This is same as the Crane Stance except that the foot back of lifted foot placed on the hollow of the other leg's knee.

Unlike the Crane Stance, this stance makes the supporting foot brake one's forward thrust and the lifted-up foot with its foot back placed on the hollow of knee helps keeping balance.

This will enable one to give variations in kick techniques, either front or sidekick.

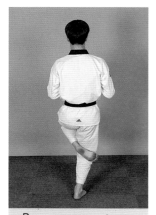

Reverse crane stance

이 서기에서 들어올린 왼쪽 무릎은 앞으로 돌출되도록 바짝 힘을 줍니다. 만약 왼쪽 무릎이 바깥으로 벌어진다면 균형 잡기가 어려울 수 있고, 다음 공격을 위한 움직임이 둔해질 것입니다.

이 서기는 균형을 유지하는 방법을 연습할 때 도움이 될 것이며, 언제든 차기를 할 준비를 갖추었기 때문에 상대방에게 혼란을 주게 됩니다.

1.2.7 오금서기

사범 학다리서기와 같으나, 다만 끌어올린 다리의 발등은 다른쪽 다리의 오금에 갖다 놓습니다.

학다리서기와 달리 이 서기는 지탱해주는 발이 앞으로 나가 지르기 하는 것을 제어하며, 들어올려진 발은 오금에 놓여진 발등과 함께 균형을 잡을 수 있게 도움을 줍니다.

이것은 앞으로 또는 옆으로 차기 기술을 할 때 변화를 주게 만듭니다.

Words

inner side 안쪽
tighten 바싹조이다
protrude 돌출하다
dull 둔한
maintenance 유지
hollow 오금, 움푹 들어간 곳

Expressions

arouse confusion 혼란을 불러일으키다
give variations 변화를 주다

1.3 Special Poom Stance

Master   While the preceding stances dealt with the techniques of keeping balance by use of two legs in various forms, the Special Poom Stances will be described by the comprehensive motion of arms, legs and the trunk which are to make harmonized stances.

To emphasize again, the 'poom' means a pose resulting from the motion taken in applying a taekwondo technique.

1.3.1 Basic Ready Stance

Master   From the Close Stance, the left foot is opened apart by one foot length.

The palms of both hands are placed to the sky. Lift both hands to the solar plexus with them almost touching your body.

Tightly clench both fists in front of the solar plexus and slightly take them down.

Halt both fists in front of the lower abdomen and breathe deep and concentrate the force at the

Basic ready stance

1.3 특수품서기

사범 지금까지 서기는 두 다리를 다양한 형태로 사용하여 중심을 잡는 기술만 언급하였으나, 특수품서기에서는 조화롭게 서기를 하기 위해 팔, 다리, 몸통을 전체적으로 사용하는 움직임으로 설명하겠습니다.

다시 강조하면, '품'이란 태권도 기술에서 쓰이는 동작의 결과로 나타나는 자세를 말합니다.

1.3.1 기본준비서기

사범 모아서기에서 왼발을 한 발 길이만큼 벌립니다.

두 손바닥은 하늘로 향하게 합니다. 두 손을 들어 몸에 거의 닿을 정도로 명치부위까지 올려줍니다.

두 주먹을 명치앞에서 꽉 쥐고 약간 아래로 내립니다.

두 주먹을 복부 아래에서 멈추고, 깊게 숨을 3분의 2 정도 내쉴 때 복부에 힘을 줍니다.

Words

comprehensive 종합적인
harmonized 조화로운
emphasize 강조하다
solar plexus 명치
clench 꽉 쥐다
breathe 숨쉬다

Expressions

dealt with~ ~을 다루다
described by ~로 설명되다
result from~ ~의 결과로 나타나다

abdomen as you exhale about two-thirds of the air.

Two fists are kept apart from each other by a fist's length and the distance between the abdomen and the fist will be kept void by a fist's length.

This is exactly a 'ready pose' as it is termed. However, it has also the meaning of a "finish up pose" to be taken at the end of movements.

The words of command for this stance will be sufficient to call just 'ready'.

Taekwondo is an art of spiritual cultivation, so it must begin with 'propriety' and end up also by 'propriety'.

To add, the truth that everything has a beginning and an ending must be kept in mind during all the movements of Taekwondo practice.

1.3.2 Fists on the Waist Ready Stance

Master   First, keep the feet as in the 'close stance'.

Place the fist on the side of the waist, each hand back facing the ground.

Fists on the waist
ready stance

두 주먹은 주먹 한 개의 간격을 두고 떨어뜨리고, 복부와 주먹 사이의 간격도 주먹 한 개 정도의 공간을 둡니다.

이것이 정확히 말 그대로 '준비자세'입니다. 그런데 준비자세는 동작 끝에 취하는 끝마무리 자세를 말하기도 합니다.

이 서기를 하기 위한 구령은 '준비'라고 하면 충분할 것 같습니다.

태권도는 정신수양을 하는 예도입니다. 그래서 태권도는 예의범절로 시작해서 예의범절로 끝나야 합니다.

부연하면, 태권도 연습의 모든 움직임 중에는 모든 것은 시작과 그 끝이 있다는 사실을 반드시 명심해야 합니다.

1.3.2 두주먹허리준비서기

사범 다리를 모아서기에서와 같이 합니다.

주먹을 허리옆에 두고 각각의 손등은 바닥을 향하게 합니다.

Words of command is enough with "Fists on the Waist Ready!", stressing the last word, "ready!"

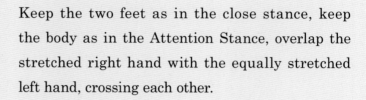 1.3.3 Overlapped Hands Ready Stance

Master   This is also used for a ready.

Keep the two feet as in the close stance, keep the body as in the Attention Stance, overlap the stretched right hand with the equally stretched left hand, crossing each other.

The fingers are stretched closed with each other, tighten the two overlapping hands but with a gap between the two by a paper's thickness,

And other things, such as the body, eyes, condition of mind and respiration control, are the same as in the 'basic ready stance'.

Words of command are "overlapped and ready!" but the last word 'ready' must be uttered loud.

1.3.4 Covered Fist Ready Stance

Master   Two feet are kept like a Close Stance,

Overlapped hands
ready stance

구령은 마지막 말인 "준비"를 강하게 하여 "두주먹허리 준비"로 하면 됩니다.

1.3.3 겹손준비서기

사범 이것도 준비에 사용되는 서기입니다.

두 발을 모아서기와 같이 하고 몸은 준비서기와 같이 하며, 뻗은 오른손을 같이 뻗은 왼손으로 서로 교차하게 하여 겹치면 됩니다.

손가락은 서로 붙여서 뻗게 하고 겹쳐진 두 손은 사이에 종이 한 장만큼의 틈만 있게 해서 밀착합니다.

그리고 몸, 눈, 마음의 상태와 호흡조절과 같은 것들은 기본준비서기와 같이 하면 됩니다.

구령은 "겹손 준비"인데요, 마지막에 "준비"는 크게 해야 합니다.

1.3.4 보주먹준비서기

사범 두 발을 모아서기와 같이 합니다.

Words

stress 강하게 발음하다
overlap 겹치다
condition 상태
respiration 호흡

Expressions

by a paper's thickness
　종이 한 장의 두께
　정도로
be uttered loud 큰 소
　리가 나게 하다

Covered fist ready stance

Pushing hands ready stance

The other body sections are kept as in the basic ready stance,

Lift the hands up to the breast and make the left hand cover the clenched right fist rolling up from the back and the left-hand thumb covers the right hand thumb.

Two arms form a circle by bending at the elbows.

The height of the hands may have three options; near philtrum, chest, the solar plexus.

This is used for a ready stance and words of command are "covered fist ready!".

1.3.5 Pushing Hands Ready Stance

Master   Stand in the parallel stance.

Keep two hands in the forms of hand blade, lift up two hands, closing them nearer with the palms upward, up to the height of the breast,

And the palms finally look face to face, and then slightly push the hands forwards with the hand blades facing the front.

몸의 다른 부위는 기본준비서기와 같이 합니다.

손을 가슴으로 올리고 왼손으로 꽉 쥔 오른손 주먹을 뒤로부터 감듯이 또는 감싸줍니다. 그리고 왼손 엄지손가락도 벌려 오른손의 엄지손가락을 감싸게 합니다.

두 팔은 팔꿈치에서 굽혀 동그랗게 만듭니다.

손 높이는 세 가지로 할 수 있습니다. 그것은 인중, 가슴, 단전입니다.

이것도 준비서기에 사용되며 구령은 "보주먹 준비"입니다.

1.3.5 통밀기준비서기

사범   나란히서기로 자세를 갖춥니다.

손을 손날과 같은 모양으로 하고, 두 손을 들어 손바닥이 위로 가게 하여 가깝게 모아서 가슴높이까지 올립니다.

그리고 손바닥끼리 마주보게 하고 손날이 앞으로 보게 하여 손을 앞으로 약간 밀어주면 됩니다.

Words

section 부위, 구획
roll up 감다, 말아올리다
philtrum 인중
parallel 평행한

Expressions

look face to face 마주보다
Keep ~ in the forms of ~ ~의 형태를 유지하다

When the hands are pushed forward, the hands must take a shape of holding a volleyball.

The hands will be slightly bent at the wrists toward the direction of thumbs and the elbows will be pushed forward at an angle of 120 degrees.

This is used for a ready stance and words of command are "pushing hands ready!", the last word 'ready' being accentuated.

2. Blocking

Master   Now we will start to learn blocking movements.

Blocking technique, along with stance, is the most basic movement.

And blocking is also the most representative technique for defense as well as grasp.

Namely, the blocking techniques are to protect oneself from being attacked by one's opponent.

Averting the opponent's attacks by escaping is another means of protecting oneself.

손을 앞으로 내밀 때에는 배구공을 잡는 모양처럼 만들어야 합니다.

손은 엄지손가락쪽으로 하여 팔목에서 약간 굽히며, 팔꿈치(팔굽)는 120도 각도로 앞으로 밀어줍니다.

이것도 준비서기에 사용되며 구령은 "통밀기 준비"인데요, 마지막 말인 "준비"를 강조합니다.

2. 막기

사범   이제 막기 동작을 배우도록 하겠습니다.

막기는 서기와 함께 가장 기본적인 동작입니다.

또한 막기는 잡기와 마찬가지로 가장 대표적인 방어 기술이기도 합니다.

막기 기술들은 상대방의 공격으로부터 자신을 보호하기 위한 것입니다.

상대방의 공격을 피해서 위기를 면하는 것은 또 다른 형태의 자기방어인 셈이죠.

Words

accentuate 강조하다
representative 대표적인
avert 피하다, 방지하다
escape 벗어나다, 달아나다

Expressions

push forward 앞으로 밀다
take a shape of ~의 형태를 취하다
start to learn 배우기 시작하다
protect oneself from~ ~로부터 자신을 보호하다

It is often said that running away from a danger is one of the best techniques for self-defense.

However it is important to master the techniques of blocking the opponent's attacks in case of a face-to-face confrontation.

A man of good defense techniques may not necessarily provoke a fight, although he is capable of winning.

Defending oneself from attacks alone could not lead to a final solution, if the other party continues attacking; therefore, it is necessary to apply the techniques of weakening the opponent's attack(offense).

That is why most defense techniques are designed to hurt the opponent while defending oneself by using the wrists or hand blades, which, if trained hard, may inflict impacts on the other party's vital points, making the latter's arms and legs incapacitated.

Therefore, defense techniques must be trained hard so that they may function equally as attacking(offensive) techniques.

자기방어를 위해서는 위험으로부터 멀리 하는 것이 최선의 기술이기도 합니다.

그러나 상대방과 직접적인 대면 상황에 있을 때 상대방의 공격을 막는 기술을 숙련시키는 것이 중요합니다.

방어 기술을 잘 갖춘 사람은 비록 이길 능력을 갖추었다고 하더라도 싸움을 유발할 필요가 없는 것이죠.

공격으로부터 자신을 방어한다고 해도 다른 사람들이 계속 공격해온다면 궁극적인 해결방안은 아닙니다. 그래서 상대방의 공격을 무력하게 하는 기술이 필요한 것입니다.

즉, 대부분의 방어 기술이 자신을 방어하는 도중에 팔목이나 손날을 사용해서 상대방에게 상처를 입히도록 고안된 이유이며, 만약 훈련이 잘 되어 있다면 다른 사람들의 팔과 다리까지 쓸모없도록 중요 부위에 타격을 가하게 되는 것입니다.

따라서 방어 기술은 제대로 익혀서 공격 기술과 같은 기능을 수행하게 해야 합니다.

Words

confrontation 대치, 대립
provoke 유발하다, 도발하다
self-defense 자기방어
inflict (괴로움을) 가하다
incapacitated 쓸모없게 되다

Expressions

run away from ~로부터 멀어지다, 도망치다
face-to-face 얼굴을 맞대고
capable of ~할 수 있다
designed to ~하도록 고안되다

With this, one may show himself or herself generously, not by winning over the opponent by initiative attacks but by overcoming the latter by mere defense techniques without impairing others.

This is indeed a righteous way if a man of virtue that Taekwondo teaches.

For that reason, Taekwondo training is planned to begin with the defense techniques, which will be followed by the training of attacking(offensive) techniques.

That is, Taekwondo never allows any initiative move of attack in its techniques.

Taekwondo uses the bodily parts, of which some are hard when contracted and sharp when opened to be applied in attacking(offensive) techniques while other solid and long parts are applied in defense techniques.

The defense is more effective when defense parts are used in a well-balanced position.

Defending with the leg or foot may be strong enough, but the remaining leg or foot has the

이러한 사실로 어떤 사람은 굳이 상대방에게 선제공격을 가해서 이기지 않더라도 약간의 방어 기술만 사용함으로써 스스로가 관대하다는 인상을 심을 수도 있는 것이죠.

이것이 바로 태권도를 배운 사람이 취할 만한 올바른 자세라 할 수 있습니다.

앞에서 살펴본 이유로, 태권도 훈련은 방어 기술부터 시작하도록 되어 있으며, 다음으로 공격 기술을 훈련하게 됩니다.

즉, 태권도는 기술을 사용함에 있어 절대 선제공격을 하지는 않는 것입니다.

태권도는 일부 신체부위는 굽히면 단단하고 펴면 날카로워 공격 기술에 사용하고, 다른 단단하고 긴 일부 신체부위는 방어 기술에 사용합니다.

방어는 방어하는 부위가 균형이 잘 갖춰진 자세에서 한다면 더 효과적입니다.

다리 또는 발로 방어하는 것은 꽤 강력할 수 있겠지만, 방어하지 않는 다리나 발은 몸의 균형을 유지하기 어려워서 어떤 기술을 제대로 수

Words

generously 관대하게
initiative attack 선제
  공격
the latter 후자
indeed 정말
righteous 옳은, 당연한
well-balanced 균형이
  잡힌

Expressions

for that reason 이런
  이유로
begin with~ ~로 시작
  하다

Wrist blocking

Hand blade blocking

Assisted blocking

Inner blocking

difficulty in keeping the balance of the body so that any mistaken technique may cause great danger.

Therefore, two arms must be always ready to render assistance. In other words, the two arms should be used in defense techniques while the legs are used to keep the balance.

It is made a rule that one of the wrists, especially the outer side of the forearm, is used for defense techniques, which is called 'Wrist Blocking'.

There is another category of blocking techniques called Hand Blade Blocking which is characterized by the sharpness of hand blade and by the weakness of deteriorated blocking power due to the wrist point.

Therefore, it is a general rule to have the other hand always accompany the main hand to assist.

The 'Wrist Blocking' is usually carried out by one wrist alone, but it may also be assisted by the other wrist, in which case the term of 'Assisted Blocking' is used.

The way of blocking can be classified as inner

행하지 못하면 큰 부상을 입을 수도 있습니다.

그래서 두 팔은 항상 보조할 수 있도록 준비해야 합니다. 부연하자면, 두 팔은 다리가 균형을 유지하는 것과 같이 방어 기술에 사용되어야 한다는 것이죠.

한쪽 팔목, 특히 팔뚝의 바깥쪽이 방어 기술에 사용된다면 '팔목막기' 라고 합니다.

손날막기라는 다른 유형의 막기 기술이 있는데요, 손날의 날카로움과 팔목 기준점 때문에 막는 강도가 약하게 되는 점이 특징입니다.

따라서 다른 손이 항상 (공격 또는 방어를 하는) 한 손을 도울 수 있도록 하는 것이 일반적인 규칙입니다.

'팔목막기'는 대개 한 팔목만으로 하게 되는데요, '거들어막기'로 수행하게 된다면 다른 팔목과 같이 사용할 수도 있습니다.

막는 방법은 안막기와 바깥막기로 분류됩니다.

Words

render (어떤 상태로) 만들다
category 유형
deteriorated 변질된
accompany 동반하다, 동행하다
classify 분류하다

Expressions

in other words 다시 말해
characterized by ~로 특징지어지다
carry out ~을 수행하다, 완수하다

Outer blocking

Face blocking

blocking (from outer side to inner side) and outer blocking (from inner side to outer side).

The starting point of defense is defined as follows:

Defense starts from the waist level to defend the face; trunk level to defend the trunk, and the shoulder level to defend the lower part(underneath). However, slightly lower or higher is permissible.

 2.1-2.6 ## 2.1 Face Blocking

Master Blocking the face by lifting up the outer-wrist is typical of Face Blocking. Of course, there are other means of blocking the face.

Face outer blocking

2.2 Face Outer Blocking

Master The outer wrist can be used for a face outer blocking. This is simply called Face Outer Blocking, because this blocking is in principle made by the outer wrist.

Inner wrist face
outer blocking

2.3 Inner Wrist Face Outer Blocking

Master The inner wrist can also be used for an outer blocking, which is called "Inner Wrist Face Outer Blocking".

방어의 시작은 다음과 같이 진행됩니다.

방어는 얼굴을 막기 위해 허리 높이에서 시작하고, 몸통을 막기 위해 몸통 높이에 맞추며, 아래를 막기 위해 어깨 높이에서 시작합니다. 이 높이는 약간 낮거나 높아도 괜찮습니다.

2.1 올려막기(얼굴막기)

사범   바깥팔목을 들어 얼굴을 막는 것이 일반적인 올려막기 형태입니다. 물론 얼굴을 막는 다른 수단들도 있습니다.

2.2 얼굴바깥막기

사범   바깥팔목이 얼굴바깥막기에 사용됩니다. 이것은 바깥팔목으로 막는 것이 원칙이기에 단순히 얼굴바깥막기라고 합니다.

2.3 얼굴안팔목바깥막기

사범   바깥막기를 위해 안팔목을 사용하는 것을 얼굴안팔목바깥막기라고 합니다.

Words

permissible 괜찮은, 허용되는
typical 일반적인, 대표적인
principle 원칙

Expressions

start from~ ~에서 시작하다
of course 물론

Face inner blocking

Trunk outer blocking

Assisting outer blocking

2.4 Face Inner Blocking

Master   The use of the inner wrist in an inner blocking is awkward and less powerful; so, the use of the outer wrist is commonplace, thereby necessitating no specification of 'outer wrist' in the term.

2.5 Trunk Outer Blocking

Master   The blocking fist must be directed toward the body and the end of the fist must be parallel with the shoulder line.

The outer hand's wrist should be situated at the waist side, the bottom of the fist kept facing upward.

The fist of the blocking arm, in the form of bending backward, is kept slightly lower (one fist's distance) than the other arm's elbow.

And the other arm is kept slightly apart from the blocking arm's shoulder, keeping the fist back directed upward from the inner side of the blocking arm.

2.6 Assisting(Guarding) Outer Blocking

Master   The fist-back of the blocking arm is kept directed

2.4 얼굴안막기

사범 안막기에서 안쪽팔목을 사용하는 것은 이상하거나 약간 힘이 적게 실릴 수 있습니다. 그래서 바깥팔목을 사용하는 것이 일반적이며, 그로 인해 '바깥팔목'이라는 용어를 굳이 명기하지 않아도 됩니다.

2.5 몸통바깥막기

사범 막는 주먹은 반드시 몸을 향해야 하며, 주먹의 끝은 어깨선과 수평이 되어야 합니다.

바깥 손의 팔목은 허리쪽에 두어야 하며, 주먹의 아래는 위를 향하게 해야 합니다.

막는 팔의 주먹은 뒤로 젖힌 형태로 다른 팔의 팔꿈치보다 약간 낮아야 합니다.

그리고 다른쪽 팔은 막는 팔의 어깨와 약간 떨어져야 하며, 막는 팔의 안쪽으로부터 주먹이 위로 향하게 해서 뒤에 위치하면 됩니다.

2.6 거들어바깥막기

사범 막는 팔의 주먹등이 몸통을 향하고, 보조해주는 팔의 주먹등이 아래

Words

awkward 어색한, 불편한
commonplace 아주 흔한
specification 설명서, 사양
situate 두다, 놓다

Expressions

less powerful 힘이 적게 실리는, 파워가 작은
apart from~ ~로부터 떨어진

toward the body and the fist-back of the assisting arm is directed downward.

The blocking hand is kept in the equal form with the Outer Wrist Trunk Blocking.

This is the same method as in the hand-blade blocking, only with its hand-blade changed into the fist.

2.7 Side Blocking

Master The side-blocking is in principle made by the inner wrist, therefore, the outer wrist must be specified in case it is used in this blocking.

The fist is kept parallel with the shoulder line, stuck to the side of the trunk.

The arm-pit is kept open at a fist's distance, the elbow looking at the side of the shoulder. The fist-back is kept looking at the side of the shoulder.

This is the same way as in the Outer-Blocking.

2.8 Underneath Blocking

Master The blocking fist is kept apart from the thigh of

를 향하게 됩니다.

막는 손은 바깥팔목몸통막기에서와 같은 형태를 유지합니다.

이것은 손날막기와 같은 방법인데요. 단지 손날이 주먹으로 바뀌는 것 뿐입니다.

2.7 옆막기

사범 옆막기는 원칙적으로 안쪽팔목으로 합니다. 그러므로 바깥팔목은 이 막기 기술에서는 역할이 구체적으로 정해져야 합니다.

주먹은 어깨선과 수평이 되어야 하며, 몸통의 옆에 밀착해야 합니다.

겨드랑이는 주먹만큼의 길이로 벌려야 하고, 팔꿈치는 어깨의 옆을 바라보게 합니다. 주먹등은 어깨의 옆을 향하도록 유지합니다.

이 기술은 바깥막기와 같은 방식입니다.

2.8 내려막기(아래막기)

사범 막는 주먹은 앞다리의 넓적다리에서 두 개의 세운 주먹 만큼의 거리

Words

equal form 같은 형태
same method 같은 방법
arm-pit 겨드랑이

Expressions

in case~ ~한 경우
keep parallel with~ ~와 수평을 유지하다

Underneath blocking

the fore-leg by the width of two erected fists.

The wrist of the other hand will rest on the waist side in the form of bending.

The blocking fist will be lifted up to the shoulder's level and the base part of the fist will face the opposite side of the face.

The other hand will be stretched toward the pit of the stomach in a state of palm down.

The elbow of the blocking arm will neither be lifted up nor stuck to the body.

2.9 Hand Blade Assisting Outer Blocking

Master   The blocking hand-blade is located in a position parallel with the lateral part of the shoulder.

The finger-tips are kept as high as the shoulder. The wrist should not be bent, the palm facing the front.

The assisting hand keeps its wrist at a position in front of the stomach pit and the hand-blade slightly apart from the body.

를 둡니다.

다른 손의 팔목은 젖힌 주먹으로 허리옆에 편히 놓습니다.

막는 주먹은 어깨 높이로 들어올리고 주먹 아래 부위는 얼굴 반대면을 향하게 합니다.

다른 손은 엎은주먹 상태로 뻗어 명치선에 오게 합니다.

막는 팔의 팔꿈치는 들어올리지 말고 몸에 붙지도 않게 해야 합니다.

2.9 손날거들어바깥막기

사범   막는 손날은 어깨의 옆 부분과 평행이 되도록 합니다.

손가락은 어깨 높이와 같게 합니다. 팔목은 굽혀지지 않게 하며, 손바닥은 정면을 향하게 합니다.

보조를 하는 손의 팔목은 명치 앞에 놓고, 손날은 몸에서 약간 떨어뜨립니다.

Words

opposite side 반대편
stomach pit 명치
lateral part 옆 부분

Expressions

rest on ~위에 놓다
neither ~ nor ~ ~도
   ~도 아니다
in parallel with~ ~와
   수평을 유지하다
face the front 정면을
   향하다
apart from~ ~부터 떨
   어져 있다

The palm of the blocking hand is kept facing upward, and the other hand keeps its palm facing backward to begin the blocking.

The finger-tips of the other hand are kept parallel with the shoulder and the wrist slightly bent is smoothly lowered, while the finger-tips of the blocking hand pass the front of the nose and the assisting hand is drawn toward the stomach.

2.10-2.10.4 2.10 Special Blocking

2.10.1 Drawing Up

Drawing up

Master   The arm, in a stance of Forward Inflection Stance, will be pulled slightly toward the side-line of the shoulder before it is drawn up to the front of the stomach-pit

Here, you may allow an open gap of an erected fist's width between the arm and the pit.

2.10.2 Mountain Shape Blocking, Wide Open Blocking

Mountain Shape blocking

Master   We go to the next 'Mountain Shape Blocking'. The expression for the term seems interesting.

막는 손의 손바닥은 위로 향하게 하며, 다른 손은 손바닥이 뒤로 향하게 하여 막기를 할 준비를 하게 합니다.

다른 손의 손가락은 어깨와 평행이 되게 하고, 팔목은 약간 굽혀서 부드럽게 아래로 하는 반면에 막는 손의 손가락은 코 앞으로 지나며, 보조해주는 손은 가슴을 향해 당깁니다.

Words

expression 표현
shape 모양, 형태
interesting 재미있는

2.10 특수막기

2.10.1 끌어올리기

사범 앞굽이 자세에서 팔이 명치앞으로 당겨지기 전에 어깨옆선을 향해 약간 끌어당깁니다.

Expressions

drawn up to ~쪽을
향해 당겨진
allow an open gap 열
린 공간을 만들다

이때 팔과 겨드랑이 사이에 세운 주먹의 너비만한 열린 공간을 만들어주세요.

2.10.2 산틀막기

사범 다음은 산틀막기인데요, '산틀'이라는 표현이 재미있어 보입니다.

In a state of blocking, the fists of both arms are kept at the height of the temple.

The base parts of the two fists will face each other along the side of the face.

2.10.3 Scissors Blocking

Scissors blocking

Master This is the form of the underneath Blocking and Wrist Outer-Blocking at the same time.

In the form of starting a low blocking, the elbow of the arm to block the trunk will be bent so that the fist is brought to the waist on the side of the hand blocking the lower part.

The two arms will cross each other simultaneously in blocking.

2.10.4 Bull Blocking

Bull blocking

Master The fists are kept apart from each other at an erected fist's width, and a gap of the same width exists between the fist and the face, too.

In the form of a basic ready stance, the two fists will lift their bases upward over the face, where

막기 상태에서 두 주먹이 관자놀이 높이에 위치하게 합니다.

두 주먹의 아래 부분들이 얼굴 측면을 따라 서로 마주보게 합니다.

Words

temple 관자놀이
scissor 가위

2.10.3 가위막기

사범   이것은 내려막기와 팔목바깥막기를 동시에 하는 기술입니다.

내려막기를 시작하려는 자세에서 몸통을 막으려는 팔의 팔굽(팔꿈치)을 굽혀서 주먹이 아래부위를 막으려는 손의 옆에 있는 허리로 향하게 합니다.

Expressions

simultaneously 동시에
at the same time 동
    시에
exist between~ ~사
    이에 위치하다

두 팔은 막을 때 서로 겹치게 하면 됩니다.

2.10.4 황소막기

사범   주먹은 서로 세운 주먹의 너비만큼 간격을 두고, 같은 간격이 주먹과 얼굴 사이에 있도록 해야 합니다.

기본 준비서기 자세에서 두 주먹의 바닥을 얼굴 위로 향해 올리며, 위에서 주먹을 비틀어서 등주먹이 앞머리를 향하게 하면 됩니다.

Face assisting side blocking

Diamond blocking

Diamond trunk blocking

the fists are twisted so that the fist-back may face the fore-head.

2.10.5 Face Assisting(Guarding) Side Blocking

Master   The blocking hand will keep its fist base directed toward the side of the face and rest beside the lateral part of the shoulder.

The assisting hand will rest in front of the chest in the form of a turned-down fist, and the arm keeps slightly aloof from the body.

2.10.6 Diamond Blocking

Master   This motion consists of Low(underneath) Blocking and Face Blocking.

At the time of a Backward-Inverted Stance, the hand blocking the lower part will be positioned above the thigh of the front foot.

2.10.7 Diamond Trunk Blocking

Master   This consists of a Face-Blocking and an inner-wrist out-blocking of the trunk.

2.10.5 얼굴거들어옆막기

사범 막는 손은 주먹의 바닥이 얼굴 측면으로 향하게 하여 어깨 측면 부위 옆에 놓습니다.

다른 손은 엎은주먹의 형태로 가슴앞에 놓고, 팔이 몸에서 약간 떨어지게 합니다.

2.10.6 금강막기

사범 이 동작은 아래막기와 얼굴막기가 합쳐서 이뤄집니다.

뒷굽이 자세에서 아래 부위를 막는 손을 앞발의 허벅지 위에 놓이게 합니다.

2.10.7 안팔목금강바깥막기

사범 이것은 얼굴막기와 안팔목몸통바깥막기가 합쳐서 이뤄집니다.

Words

twist 비틀다
beside ~ 옆에
hinge 돌쩌귀, 경첩

Expressions

keep slightly aloof
  from~ ~에서 약간
  떨어지게 하다
consist of~ ~로 구성
  되다

In the stance of Small Hinge, the two arms are drawn toward the chest to conduct both face-blocking and inner-wrist out-blocking of the trunk simultaneously.

For a Diamond Blocking, it is essential that a face-blocking and another blocking are conducted simultaneously.

2.10.8 Hand Blade Diamond Blocking

Hand blade diamond blocking

Master   This technique is the same as in the Diamond blocking, except that the hand-blade is used this time.

2.10.9 Crane Diamond Blocking

Crane diamond blocking

Master   This is an action having done Diamond Blocking in th Crane Stance.

The lower part blocking hand will rest in front of the lateral part of the trunk.

작은돌쩌귀 자세에서 두 팔을 가슴쪽으로 하여 올려막기와 안팔목바깥막기를 동시에 하는 것입니다.

금강막기를 할 때에는 올려막기와 다른 막기 기술이 반드시 동시에 이뤄져야 합니다.

2.10.8 손날금강막기

사범 이 기술은 금강막기와 같은 방식인데요, 손날이 사용된다는 점이 다릅니다.

2.10.9 학다리금강막기

사범 이것은 학다리서기에서 금강막기를 하는 동작입니다.

손을 막는 아래 부위가 몸통의 옆 측면에 놓이게 됩니다.

glabella
(미간)

philtrum
(인중)

crown(정수리)

temple(관자놀이)

uvula(목젖)

epigastrium
(명치)

testis
(고환)

shin(정강이)

Vital point of human body

3. Punch(Punching)

Master From now on, we will learn about some attack (offense) techniques.

The first attack(offense) technique to learn is a punch. It is to punch the opponent's vital point or target.

Disciple Master, if we punch the opponent's vital point, it will then be fatal. Are there any regulations or taboo subjects?

Master Yes, there are a couple of basic regulations. First, two fists should be laid on both sides of the waist line with its palm upward.

Next, reverse the fist and then stretch the arm to fold out the elbow part.

Finally, you should make the fist as soon as it reaches the target.

Disciple Then which part of the body could be the main target for this technique?

3. 지르기

사범 오늘부터는 몇 가지 공격 기술을 배우기 시작하겠습니다.

첫 번째 공격 기술은 지르기입니다. 이것은 주먹으로 상대방의 급소나 목표를 지르는 것을 말합니다.

문하생 사범님, 주먹으로 급소를 가격하면 치명적일 것 같은데요. 어떤 규칙이나 금기사항이 있나요?

사범 네, 몇 가지 기본규칙이 있는데요. 첫째로, 지르기 직전의 두 주먹은 양쪽 허리 윗부분에서 손등이 밑을 향하도록 젖혀야 합니다.

다음으로 주먹을 뒤엎으며 팔꿈치부위가 완전히 펴지도록 팔을 힘껏 뻗습니다.

마지막으로 지른 주먹이 목표에 닿으면 절도 있게 빨리 당겨야 합니다.

사범 그럼 어느 부위를 주로 목표로 해야 하는가요?

Words

vital point 급소
fatal 치명적인
regulation 규칙
taboo subject 금기사항

Expressions

learn about~ ~에 대해 배우다
fold out 펴지다, 열리다

Master   Mainly the opponent's face and chest. Are you ready for training now?

Disciple   Yes, we are.

 3.1 Method

Master   The punch is divided into 'Right Punch' and 'Opposite Punch' according to the position of the attacker's foot.

3.1.1 Right Punch

Right punch

Master   When the feet are widely opened fore and back due to the movement of body weight, a Right Punch is performed by the fist on the side of the back foot.

There are a Fist-Punch, an Erected Fist Punch and a Bending Fist-Punch.

The pulling fist will be pulled back through the same line with the target of the punching fist.

3.1.2 Opposite Punch

Opposite punch

Master   An Opposite Punch is applied by the fist on the fore foot side, in the same situation as the above.

사범   상대방의 얼굴과 가슴입니다. 이제 시작해 볼까요?

문하생   네, 준비되었습니다.

3.1 방법

사범   지르기는 공격자의 발 위치에 따라 "바로지르기"와 "반대지르기"로 구분됩니다.

3.1.1 바로지르기

사범   몸의 중심 이동 때문에 양 발이 앞뒤로 넓게 벌려 있을 때 뒷발이 있는 쪽에서 주먹으로 바로지르기를 합니다.

바로지르기에는 주먹지르기, 세운주먹지르기, 젖힌주먹지르기가 있습니다.

잡아당기는 주먹은 지르기 주먹의 목표물과 동일선상으로 당깁니다.

3.1.2 반대지르기

사범   반대지르기는 바로지르기와 같이 앞발 쪽에 있는 주먹으로 수행합니다.

Words

position 위치
widely 넓게
body weight 체중

Expressions

divided into~ ~로 구분된다. ~로 나누어지다
fore and back 앞뒤로
through the same line with~ ~와 동일선상으로

The fist on the side of the fore foot is used for a punch and there are a Fist Punch, an Erected Fist Punch and a Bending Fist Punch.

The pulling fist will be pulled back through the same line with the target of the punching fist.

3.1.3 Erected(Vertical) Punch

Erected punch

Master A punch is made by an erected fist (the thumb facing upward).

This is used when an opponent is within a close distance, keeping the elbow in a state of bending.

3.1.4 Bending Backward Punch

Bending backward punch

Master A punch is made by the fist bent backward. This is applied to the opponent's body(trunk) in a close distance.

At the time of punching, the fist-back fist faces downward, the elbow being bent at an angle within 120 degrees.

If the elbow is fully stretched out for a punching against an opponent far away, the power decreases

앞발 쪽에 있는 주먹으로 지르기를 하며, 주먹지르기, 세운주먹지르기, 젖힌주먹지르기가 있습니다.

당기는 주먹은 지르기 주먹의 목표물과 동일선상으로 당겨야 합니다.

3.1.3 세워지르기

사범 세워지르기는 엄지손가락을 위로 향하게 하여 세운 주먹으로 지르기합니다.

이 기술은 상대방이 가까운 거리에 있을 때 팔꿈치를 굽힌 상태로 하는 것입니다.

3.1.4 젖혀지르기

사범 뒤로 젖힌 주먹으로 하는 지르기입니다. 이 기술은 가까운 거리에 있는 상대방의 몸(몸통)을 공격합니다.

지르기 하는 순간 등주먹은 아래로 향하고, 팔꿈치는 120도 이내로 굽혀져 있게 됩니다.

멀리 떨어져 있는 상대방에게 지르기 하기 위해 팔꿈치가 완전히 펴져 있다면 힘이 줄어들어 지르기가 바로지르기 또는 반대지르기에 비

Words

vertical 수직의, 세로의
thumb 엄지, 무지
decrease 줄어들다

Expressions

within a close distance
    가까운 거리에 있는
in a state of~ ~의 상
    태에 있는

Upward punch

and the punching will be weaker than a Right Punch or an Opposite Punch.

Master   If the fist reaches the opponent's face, then it is called Upward Punch.

 3.2 Target

Master   Punch techniques are varied depending on the target parts of the opponent.

At the time of practicing or engaging in a face to face Kyorugi, one must always have in mind an imaginary opponent or the target point.

Generally, in the training of basic movements or Poomsae, one practices attack or defense techniques with no real opponent.

Therefore, one must always draw in mind an opponent before him or her whose physical conditions and level of techniques are like his or her.

3.2.1 Face Punch

Face punch

Master   The philtrum is the typical target point in the face for punch.

해 약해질 것입니다.

만약 주먹이 상대방의 얼굴을 가격하게 된다면 치지르기라고 합니다.

Words
practice 실습하다
engage (행위를) 하다
imaginary 가상의, 상상의

3.2 목표

사범　목표부위가 어디인가에 따라 지르기를 분류하기도 합니다.

일 대 일 겨루기를 할 때에는 반드시 마음에 가상의 상대 또는 목표부위를 염두에 두어야 합니다.

Expressions
be weaker 약해지다
depending on~ ~에 따라
at the time of~ ~를 할 때

기본동작이나 품새를 훈련할 때에는 실전 상대 없이 공격 또는 방어 기술들을 연습하게 됩니다.

따라서 훈련하는 사람의 체격조건과 기술수준이 비슷한 가상의 상대방을 항상 염두에 두어야만 하는 것이죠.

3.2.1 얼굴지르기

사범　지르기에서 일반적인 얼굴의 목표부위는 인중입니다.

The way of punching is identical with that of a Trunk Punch (see the next).

3.2.2 Trunk Punch

Trunk punch

Master   The solar plexus is the typical point of attack in the trunk.

The shoulder is kept wide open and the wrist of punching fist will rest on the waist, the elbow sticking spontaneously to the body.

The arm-pit is kept closed, the fist of the opposite side is pulled rapidly with the maximum use of the repulsive power of the waist, and at the same time a punching is directed toward the height of the solar plexus at the right center of the shoulders of both sides.

The pulling fist is drawn back rapidly on the straight line with the solar plexus.

3.2.3 Low(Underneath) Punch

Low punch

Master   The lower part of the abdomen is the typical point of target in the lower part of the body.

지르기 방법은 몸통지르기와 같습니다(다음 참조).

3.2.2 몸통지르기

사범 몸통에서는 명치가 일반적인 공격부위입니다.

어깨는 넓게 펴고, 지르기 주먹의 팔목은 허리에 편히 갖다 대며, 팔꿈치는 몸에 부드럽게 갖다 붙입니다.

겨드랑이는 벌리지 말고, 반대편에 있는 주먹은 허리의 반발력을 최대한 이용하여 빨리 끌어당기며, 양쪽 어깨의 오른편 중앙을 명치 높이에 맞춰 지르기를 합니다.

끌어당기는 주먹은 명치와 일직선으로 재빨리 잡아당깁니다.

3.2.3 아래지르기

사범 하체에서는 단전이 일반적인 공격부위입니다.

Words

identical 동일한, 똑같은
spontaneously 자연스럽게, 자발적으로
repulsive power 반발력
rapidly 재빠르게

Expressions

keep wide open 넓게 벌려진 상태를 유지하다
drawn back 잡아당겨진

Side punch

Downward punch

Spiral punch

The way of punch equals with a Trunk Punch.

3.3 Direction

Master   Also, types of punch are varied according to its direction.

3.3.1 Side Punch

Master   One delivers a punch to the opponent's side.

3.3.2 Downward Punch

Master   One punches downward at the bottom of the opponent.

3.3.3 Spiral(Turning) Punch

Master   The fist does not stretch straight as it is but half spirals before reaching the target from the waist.

This is used when the opponent is closer and the elbow bend a little.

지르기 방법은 몸통지르기와 같습니다.

3.3 방향

사범   방향에 따라서도 종류가 변합니다.

Words

deliver 가지고 가다
bottom 바닥

3.3.1 옆지르기

사범   상대방의 옆구리에 지르기를 합니다.

3.3.2 내려지르기

사범   상대방의 몸통 아래로 지르기를 합니다.

Expressions

equal with ~와 같다
according to ~에 따
  라
stretch straight 곧게
  뻗치다

3.3.3 돌려지르기

사범   주먹을 곧바로 뻗지 않고 허리에서부터 목표물에 닿기 전에 반 정도
만 돌리듯 회전합니다.

이 기술은 상대방이 가까이 있고 팔꿈치가 약간 접혀 있을 때 사용합
니다.

Upward punch

3.3.4 Upward Punch

Master Usually a punch is delivered to the opponent's jaw by the fist thrusting straightly upward from the waist, in which the back of fist faces the opponent, the elbow slightly bending.

3.4 Target and Method

Master So far, we have seen the standard forms of punch, but there are applied techniques of punch with the specific terms.

3.4.1 Face Right Punch & Face Opposite Punch

Master The same as the face punch.

3.4.2 Trunk Opposite Punch

Master The fist on the fore-foot side executes a punch so that it is laid on the straight line with the pit of the stomach.

Point of attention is that it is the same as the Trunk Punch.

3.3.4 치지르기

사범 일반적으로 주먹이 허리에서부터 위로 일직선으로 찌르듯이 상대방의 턱을 지르기 하며, 허리에서 주먹의 등은 상대방을 향하고 팔꿈치는 약간 접혀 있습니다.

3.4 목표와 방법

사범 지금까지는 지르기의 표준형태를 살펴보았는데요, 특정 용어(동작)를 사용한 지르기 응용기술들도 있습니다.

3.4.1 얼굴바로지르기와 얼굴반대지르기

사범 얼굴지르기와 같은 방식입니다.

3.4.2 몸통반대지르기

사범 앞발쪽에 위치한 주먹으로 지르기를 하며, 명치와 같은 일직선에 놓이게 합니다.

주목할 점은 이것이 몸통지르기와 같은 방식이라는 점입니다.

Words

execute (동작을) 해내다, 수행하다
attention 주목, 주의

Expressions

specific term 특정 용어
the same as~ ~와 같다
lay on ~에 놓다
pit of the stomach 명치

4. Hit(Hitting, Strike, Striking)

Master   Second attack(offense) technique to learn is a hit.

What is this hit technique about? Anyone who can explain?

Disciple   It must be the one with hand. Not more in details, sorry.

Master   That's good. It is basically all the attack techniques with hand except using the right fist and fingertip.

Disciple   Then, should we stretch the elbow? Otherwise, could we also bend it?

Master   Both applicable. You may also hit the target with turning force.

Disciple   I see. Let's try it then.

Master   If an attack is enacted by the use of spinning force of the body or the fist moves in a circle with the elbow either inflected or stretched to inflict impact on a target, it is called 'hit'.

4. 치기

사범 두 번째 공격 기술은 치기입니다.

치기는 어떤 동작일까요? 설명할 수 있으신가요?

문하생 분명 손을 사용하는 동작일 텐데요. 자세히는 모르겠습니다.

사범 손의 모든 공격기술은 맞는데요. 바른주먹과 손끝을 사용하지 않는 것입니다.

문하생 그럼 팔꿈치(팔굽)를 펴야 하는 건가요. 아니면 굽혀도 되는 건가요?

사범 두 가지 다 해도 됩니다. 또한 회전력을 주어 목표물을 가격해도 되는 것이죠.

문하생 그렇군요. 그럼 해보도록 하죠.

사범 만약 몸의 회전력으로 공격을 하거나 목표물을 타격하기 위해 팔꿈치를 굽히거나 뻗어서 주먹을 원을 그리며 옮길 경우 '치기'라고 합니다.

Words

explain 설명하다
turning force(spinning force) 회전력
basically 기본적으로

Expressions

in details 자세히
move in a circle 원을 그리며 움직이다

There are various types of hits and they are largely termed in accordance with the way of motions by the applied bodily parts toward the targets.

4.1 Front Hit

Front hit

Master   The parts of the fore(index) finger and the middle finger on the back fist are employed.

The wrist on the side of the hitting back fist should not be bent.

The hitting back fist with its fist-back facing upward is lifted up brushing past the arm-pit over the waist on the opposite side to make a hitting by bending the back fist at the height of the philtrum.

4.2 Face Outer Hit

Face outer hit

Master   The same way as in the outer-blocking, but the hit is made against the targets of the lateral jaw and the head temple.

The back fist is erected to the height of the philtrum to deliver a hit.

치기에는 다양한 유형이 있으며, 그것들은 대개 목표물을 향해 몸이 어떻게 쓰이는지에 따라 움직임의 방식에 맞춰 이름이 정해집니다.

Words

employ 사용하다
philtrum 인중
head temple 관자놀이

4.1 앞치기

사범 주먹등의 집게손가락과 가운데손가락의 첫 번째마디가 사용됩니다.

치기를 하는 등주먹쪽에 있는 팔목이 굽혀지면 안 됩니다.

치는 등주먹을 주먹등이 위로 향하게 하여 반대편 허리 위에서 겨드랑이를 스치며 올려 인중 높이로 등주먹을 젖혀 칩니다.

Expressions

in accordance with~
  ~에 맞추어
fore(index) finger 집
  게손가락

4.2 얼굴바깥치기

사범 바깥막기와 같은 방식이지만, 턱 측면과 관자놀이를 목표로 하는 치기입니다.

치기를 하기 위해 등주먹을 인중 높이로 올립니다.

Side hit

4.3-4.8 4.3 Side Hit

Master   Side hit will aim to the target right beside you.

4.4 Trunk Side Hit

Master   The hitting arm stretches on the same line with the body's sideward line.

At the time of Trunk Outer Hit, the attacker's body turns sideways by 45 degrees and the arm forms an angle, the opponent standing in front.

4.5 Trunk Downward Hit

Master   This action has the primary purpose of blocking rather than an attack(offense).

The fist-back makes a downward hit passing through the trunk by means of bending itself.

The back fist making a hit keeps its fist-back face upward at the height of the ear on the opposite side

And then the back fist bends itself downward to make a hit, at the same time when the other hand is pulled back after it has been lightly stretched forward.

4.3 옆치기

사범   바로 옆쪽에 있는 목표물을 가격하는 기술입니다.

Words

beside ~의 옆에
primary 주된, 일차적
  인

4.4 몸통옆치기

사범   치기를 하는 팔이 몸의 옆 방향선과 같은 동선에서 뻗게 합니다.

몸통바깥치기를 할 때 공격하는 사람의 몸이 측면으로 45도 돌아 상
대방이 앞에 서 있을 때 팔이 (어깨에서) 각을 이루게 합니다.

Expressions

aim to ~을 목표로 하다
on the same line with
  ~와 같은 선상에서
form an angle 각을
  이루다
pass through~ ~을
  지나다
on the opposite side
  반대쪽에 있는

4.5 몸통내려치기

사범   이 치기는 공격보다는 막기에 중점을 둔 것입니다.

주먹등을 굽히면서 몸통을 지나 내려치기를 합니다.

치기를 하는 등주먹은 주먹등 표면을 반대쪽에 있는 귀 높이로 하여
올립니다.

그리고 나서 다른 손을 가볍게 앞으로 뻗은 상태에서 당김과 동시에
아래로 젖혀서 치기를 합니다.

4.6 Low(Underneath) Downward Hit

Master   This hit is usually used in the breaking techniques.

4.7 Hammer Fist Target Hit

Hammer fist target hit

Master   A target is formed when the target hand keeps its thumb opened.

At a target hitting by a hammer fist, the fist hits the palm of the target hand.

The target hand should not grasp the hitting fist.

4.8 Hammer Fist Low(Beneath) Target Hit

Hammer fist low target hit

Master   The two arms are kept open from each other at the upper side and then brought down to the front of the lower abdomen to deliver a target hit with a hammer-fist.

The two arms conducting a target hit will not be completely unfolded.

There is a gap of an erected fist's width between the target hitting hand and the lower abdomen.

4.6 아래내려치기

사범 이 치기는 주로 격파를 할 때 사용됩니다.

4.7 메주먹표적치기

사범 목표물이 되는 손의 엄지손가락을 벌려 목표물로 삼습니다.

메주먹으로 목표물을 칠 때 주먹이 목표물이 되는 손의 손바닥을 치게 됩니다.

목표가 되는 손은 치기를 하는 주먹을 잡아서는 안 됩니다.

4.8 아래메주먹표적치기

사범 두 팔은 위에서 서로 열린 채로 있고. 메주먹으로 목표물을 치기 위해 복부 아래의 앞쪽으로 내립니다.

목표물을 치는 두 팔은 완전히 펼쳐지지 않게 합니다.

목표물을 치는 손과 복부 아래 사이에 있는 세운 주먹 사이에는 간격이 있어야 합니다.

Words
breaking technique
 격파
grasp (꽉) 쥐다
completely 완전히
unfold 펼치다

Expressions
keep opened 벌려져
 있게 하다
each other 서로

4.9-4.15 4.9 Hand Blade Face Front Hit

Hand blade face front hit

Master   A curved hand-blade executes a neck-hitting.

The other hand will be extended forward and it is pulled back to be laid on the waist when a neck-hitting is made.

4.10 Palm Hand Face Inner Hit

Master   The finger-tips of a palm hand will face upward and then they will be leaned sideways by an angle of 45 degrees to make a front hitting.

4.11 Arc Hand Face Front Hit

Arc hand face front hit

Master   The Palm Hand Jaw Hit and 'Kaljaebi' are carried out in a straight-line motion as in the punch.

But they are termed 'hit' because the applied bodily parts are wide and long.

The Arc Hand is used in Kaljaebi to attack target and types of attack are varied according to target parts.

Hitting the neck: one attacks the gullet region

4.9 손날얼굴앞치기

사범 굽혀진 손날로 목치기를 하는 것입니다.

다른 손은 앞으로 뻗어 있어야 하며, 목치기를 할 때 허리에 놓일 수 있도록 당겨야 합니다.

4.10 얼굴바탕손앞치기

사범 바탕손의 손가락이 위로 향하고, 손가락이 앞치기를 하기 위해 45도 각을 이루도록 옆으로 비스듬히 눕힙니다.

4.11 얼굴아금손앞치기(칼재비)

사범 턱바탕손앞치기와 칼재비는 지르기와 같이 직선 운동을 합니다.

그러나 두 기술은 '치기'로 분류되는데요, 사용하는 신체부위가 넓거나 길기 때문입니다.

칼재비는 아금손으로 목표를 공격하며, 목표부위에 따라 공격방법이 다릅니다.

목치기 : 지르기에서와 같이 팔을 직선으로 뻗어 아금손으로 식도부

Words

curved 굽혀진
execute (동작을) 해내
다, 수행하다

Expressions

in a straight-line 직전
으로

with the Arc Hand by stretching the arm straight as in the punch.

Bending the knee: grasp a back sole with a hand and attack the knee with an arc hand.

4.12 Bent Wrist Jaw Hit

Bent Wrist jaw hit

Master   This is mainly used in defense.

4.13 Pincers Wrist Hit

Pincers wrist hit

Master   This is principally used in attacking(offending) the neck like the Arc Hand.

4.14 Elbow Raise-Up Hit

Elbow raise-up hit

Master   The elbow making a raise-up hitting is raised upward skimming the arm-pit.

The back of the hand looks sideways and the waist is twisted at the time of hitting.

4.15 Elbow Spiral(Turning) Hit

Master   The back of the hand looks upward and the elbow is turned to the maximum to be in front of the shoulder.

위를 공격합니다.

무릎꺾기 : 한 손으로 (발의) 뒤축을 잡고, 아금손으로 무릎을 공격
합니다.

Words

mainly(principally) 주
로
skim (표면을) 스치듯
하며 지나가다

4.12 턱굽힌손목올려치기

사범   이 기술은 방어에 주로 사용됩니다.

4.13 집게주먹치기

사범   이것은 주로 아금손과 같이 목을 공격할 때 쓰입니다.

Expressions

to the maximum 최
대로
at the time of~ ~할 때

4.14 팔굽올려치기

사범   올려치기를 하는 팔굽이 겨드랑이를 스치듯이 위로 올려칩니다.

손등이 옆면을 향하게 하며, 칠 때 허리를 틀어줍니다.

4.15 팔굽돌려치기

사범   손등이 위로 향하게 하고, 팔굽을 최대한 어깨 앞쪽으로 오도록 돌려
줍니다.

Elbow spiral hit

The elbow is positioned at a point higher than the shoulder line and the waist is twisted at the time of hitting.

4.16 Elbow Side Hit

Master   In a riding stance, the fist of hitting side is brought to the shoulder line on the opposite side to touch the opposite hand's palm, and then the elbow makes a lateral hitting, making profit of the power of pushing by the opposite hand.

The finger-tips of the opposite hand look upward and they do not grab the fist.

And the opposite hand is positioned in front of the chest on the hitting elbow's side

4.17 Elbow Target Hit

Master   The hand on the opposite side is opened to become a target and the elbow of the attacking arm hits the target.

The target does not move and the elbow moves to make a hitting.

Elbow target hit

팔굽이 어깨선보다 위쪽에 위치하게 하며, 칠 때 허리를 틀어줍니다.

Words

position ~에 위치하
다, 자리잡다
grab 쥐다, 잡다

4.16 팔굽옆치기

사범   주춤서기에서 상대방의 손바닥에 닿기 위해 상대방쪽에 있는 어깨선
으로 치는 쪽의 주먹이 향하게 하며, 반대손이 밀어주는 힘을 이용하
여 팔굽을 옆으로 치면 됩니다.

반대편에 있는 손의 손끝은 위로 향하게 하고, 주먹을 잡지 않습니다.

Expressions

make profit 이득을 얻
다, ~를 이용하다
on the opposite side
반대편에서

그리고 반대편에 있는 손은 치기를 하는 팔굽쪽의 가슴앞에 위치시
키면 됩니다.

4.17 팔굽표적치기

사범   반대쪽에 있는 손은 목표물이 되도록 펴주며, 공격하는 팔의 팔굽으
로 목표물을 치면 됩니다.

목표물은 움직이지 않고, 팔굽이 치기 위해 따라갑니다.

The thumb of the target hand is stuck to the fore(index) finger and it should not grab the elbow.

4.18 Knee Raise–Up Hit

Knee raise-up hit

Master   One leg supports the body and the other leg's knee is bent to be lifted up for a hit.

The waist is lightly curved and the ankle rests in a natural state.

4.19 Knee Spiral(Turning) Hit

Knee spiral hit

Master   As one leg supports the body, the other leg is raised up by bending the knee to execute a knee spiral(turning) hit.

It will be good if one hand pulls and drags in some part of the opponent's body so that the other hand may execute a hit.

목표가 되는 손의 엄지손가락은 집게손가락에 붙이고, 팔굽을 잡으면
안 됩니다.

4.18 무릎올려치기

사범   한쪽 다리는 몸을 지탱해주며, 다른 쪽의 무릎은 굽혀서 들어올려 치
기를 합니다.

허리는 가볍게 굽히고 발목은 자연스럽게 해줍니다.

4.19 무릎돌려치기

사범   한쪽 다리로 몸을 지탱하며, 다른 쪽의 다리는 무릎을 굽혀 들어올려
돌려치기를 합니다.

한 손으로 상대방의 신체부위를 잡고 끌어당기면 다른 손이 치기를
하는 데 도움이 될 것입니다.

Words

clench 쥐다
ankle-bones 발목뼈

Expressions

stick to~ ~에 붙이다
locate on ~에 위치
　하다
raise up 들어올리다

5. Thrusting

Master We will learn to know about thrusting as the third attack(offense) technique following punch and hit.

Thrusting techniques can be performed in the same way as punch techniques.

The only difference is that their applied bodily parts are not the fist but the fingertips.

By a finger's length, thrusting techniques enable to pierce deeper and longer to a more distanced target.

On the contrary, if the finger joints are not hard enough by training, they can be broken easily.

5.1 Flat Hand Tips Erected(Vertical) Thrusting

Flat hand tips
erected thrusting

Master This technique aims mainly at the opponent's solar plexus.

The elbow of the hand making the Flat Hand Tips Thrusting stays over the hand back of the other hand.

5. 찌르기

사범   지르기, 치기에 이어 세 번째 공격 기술인 찌르기에 대해 알아보겠습니다.

찌르기 기술은 지르기 기술과 같은 방식으로 수행합니다.

한 가지 차이점은 사용하는 신체부위가 주먹이 아닌 손가락끝이라는 것입니다.

손가락의 길이 때문에 찌르기 기술은 멀리 떨어져 있는 목표물을 더 깊고 길게 찌를 수 있습니다.

반대로, 손가락관절이 훈련을 통해 충분히 단단해져 있지 않다면 관절이 쉽게 부러질 수도 있습니다.

5.1 편손끝세워찌르기

사범   이 기술은 주로 상대방의 명치를 목표로 합니다.

편손끝찌르기를 하는 손 쪽에 있는 팔굽이 다른 손의 손등 위에 놓입니다.

Words

difference 차이
pierce 찌르다
solar plexus 명치

Expressions

in the same way as~
   ~와 같은 방법으로
deeper and longer 더
   깊고 더 길게
on the contrary 반대
   로

Then the Flat Hand Tips Thrusts straight forward in parallel with the height of the solar plexus.

In a state in which the other hand is unfolded and extended forward, make the elbow bent with the fingertips looking upward.

As a final movement, execute the Palm Pushing Defense and Flat Hand Tips Thrusting from the waist simultaneously.

5.2 Flat Hand Tips Turn Over Thrusting

Master   Flat Hand Tips Thrust with its hand back directing upward.

This technique is mainly used in attacking the opponent's eyes, neck and solar plexus.

Its underneath attacking is not that effective.

5.3 Flat Hand Tips Bending Backward Thrusting

Master   This technique is mainly used in attacking the opponent's rib, solar plexus, groin, etc.

The fingertips will look downward while the palm

Flat hand tips
turn over thrusting

그리고 편손끝은 명치의 높이에 맞게 일직선으로 앞으로 찌릅니다.

반대손이 펼쳐지고 앞으로 뻗어 있는 상태에서 손가락을 위로 보게 하면서 팔굽이 굽혀지게 합니다.

마지막 동작으로 손바닥눌러막기와 허리에서부터 편손끝찌르기를 동시에 하면 됩니다.

Words
final 마지막
rib 늑골, 갈비뼈
groin 사타구니(서혜부)

5.2 편손끝엎어찌르기

사범   찌르는 손등이 위를 향하게 하여 손끝으로 찌릅니다.

Expressions
in parallel with~ ~와 수평으로
in a state ~한 상태에서

이 기술은 주로 상대방의 눈, 목, 명치를 공격할 때 사용합니다.

몸통 이하는 찔러도 효과가 별로 없습니다.

5.3 편손끝젖혀찌르기

사범   이 기술은 상대방의 늑골, 명치, 사타구니 등을 공격할 때 쓰입니다.

손바닥쪽이 위를 향하는 반면, 손가락끝은 아래쪽을 보게 됩니다.

Flat hand tips bending
backward thrusting

Scissors hand tips thrusting

Single hand tips thrusting

Combined two hand
tips Thrusting

side will face upward.

The opposite hand, whose base part looks toward the face, is raised up to the level of the shoulder.

Let the hand making a thrusting stay on the waist with its palm facing upward.

And the opposite hand is extended forward, with its back looking upward.

 5.4-5.9 **5.4 Scissors Hand Tips Thrusting**

Master This is mainly used in attacking the opponent's two eyes at a time.

The palm is kept facing downward.

5.5 Single Hand Tips Thrusting

Master Mainly one eye becomes target at the Single Hand Tips Thrusting.

5.6 Combined(Joint) Two Hand Tips Thrusting

Master Compared with Single Hand Tip, Two Hand Tips Thrusting will exert more force.

손바닥이 얼굴을 향하고 있는 반대쪽의 손은 어깨 높이까지 올려줍니다.

Words

opposite 반대쪽
thrust 찌르다

찌르기를 하고 있는 손은 손바닥이 위를 향하게 하여 옆구리에 둡니다.

그리고 반대쪽 손은 손등이 위를 보게 하여 앞으로 뻗습니다.

5.4 가위손끝찌르기

사범 이것은 상대방의 두 눈을 동시에 공격할 때 사용합니다.

Expressions

to the level of~ ~의 높이까지
at a time 동시에
compare with ~와 비교하다
exert more force 더 많은 힘을 주다

손바닥은 아래쪽을 향하게 유지합니다.

5.5 한손끝찌르기

사범 한손끝찌르기에서는 주로 상대방의 눈이 공격 대상입니다.

5.6 모은두손끝찌르기

사범 한손끝과 비교하여 두손끝지르기는 더 많은 힘을 가할 수 있을 것입니다.

This technique aims at the opponent's eyes, neck and solar plexus.

5.7 Combined(Joint) Three Hand Tips Thrusting

Combined three hand tips thrusting

Master   Here, targets are the same as the two fingertips attack.

5.8 Combined(Joint) All Hand Tips Pounding

Combined all hand tips pounding

Master   Five fingertips together will make a powerful attack almost like the fist.

But this technique can carry out downward or inward attack only because it cannot make a straight motion like thrusting.

5.9. Crane Stance Thrusting

Crane Stance thrusting

Master   This technique thrusts forward and one takes the posture of Crane Stance.

Simultaneously, one hand performs Pressing Defense while the other hand executes Flat Hand Tips Erected(vertical) Thrusting.

이 기술은 상대방의 눈, 목, 명치를 공격 목표로 하게 됩니다.

5.7 모은세손끝찌르기

사범   이 기술에서 목표물은 두손끝 공격과 같습니다.

5.8 모둠손끝찍기

사범   다섯손가락끝은 주먹과 거의 비슷한 강력한 힘을 발휘할 것입니다.

그런데 이 기술은 찌르기와 같은 직선동작을 하지 않기 때문에 아래 또는 안쪽 방향의 공격을 수행할 수 있습니다.

5.9 학다리서기찌르기

사범   이 기술은 앞으로 찌르면서 학다리서기 자세를 취합니다.

동시에 한 손은 눌러막기를 하고, 다른 손은 편손끝세워찌르기를 수행합니다.

Words

simultaneously 동시에
perform 행하다

Expressions

make a powerful attack 강한 공격을 하다
carry out 수행하다

6. Kick (Kicking)

Master   As the fourth attack(offense) technique, let us learn about a kick.

Kick, together with the throwing down technique, is the most representative basic technique that uses the foot.

Kick has somehow stronger force than punch by fist as it will use foot.

6.1 Front Kick

Front kick

Master   First, raise the folded knee of the kicking leg up to the breast and immediately push the foot forward, fully stretching the leg.

The track of foot must be on a straight line toward the target.

The target must be kicked by the fore sole, the toes bending outward. The groin, lower part of abdomen, solar plexus, etc, are the targets.

6. 차기

사범   네 번째 공격기술로 차기에 대해 배워보겠습니다.

차기는 넘기기 기술과 더불어 발을 사용하는 대표적인 기본기술입니다.

아무래도 발을 사용하므로 주먹으로 지르기보다 훨씬 큰 위력을 가지고 있습니다.

6.1 앞차기

사범   먼저 차려고 하는 다리쪽의 무릎을 굽혀 가슴높이까지 올리고 난 후에 즉시 다리를 완전히 펴서 발을 앞으로 내밀면 됩니다.

발의 궤적은 목표물을 향해 일직선상에 놓여야 합니다.

목표물은 발끝이 바깥쪽으로 접히게 하여 반드시 앞축으로 차야 합니다. 낭심. 복부 아래. 명치 등이 공격 목표가 됩니다.

Words

representative 대표적인
somehow 훨씬
immediately 즉시
fully 완전히, 최대로

Expressions

on a straight line 일직선상에
kick leg up 다리를 차올리다

6.2 Side Kick

Side kick

Master   As in the Front Kick, one lifts up the kicking leg, folding the knee, and then stretches the folded knee as he or she turns the body in the opposite direction to the target. And, finally, kick the target with the back sole of foot.

After the kick, the kicking leg will be drawn back to the original position or where it is intended to be placed.

6.3 Spiral(Turning) Kick

Spiral kick

Master   Spiral Kick is also called 'roundhouse kick' where the term 'roundhouse' means 'big swinging punch at the side of body' in Boxing game.

First, putting the weight on the pivoting foot, one turns the body immediately after folding the knee.

Then, as the knee stretches, makes the kicking foot circle horizontally so that the fore sole may kick the target.

The supporting leg stretches its ankle and knee to help the fore sole pivot the body easily.

6.2 옆차기

사범 앞차기에서와 같이 차고자 하는 발을 들고 무릎을 굽히고 목표물을 향해 반대쪽으로 몸을 돌리면서 굽힌 무릎을 뻗습니다. 마지막으로 발의 뒤축(발날)으로 목표물을 차면 됩니다.

Words
finally 마지막으로
term 용어
horizontally 수평으로

차기를 한 후에 차기를 한 다리는 다시 원래 자리, 또는 위치하게 하려는 곳으로 돌아오게 합니다.

6.3 돌려차기

사범 돌려차기는 권투에서 쓰이는 '옆으로 크게 휘둘러 치는 펀치'를 뜻하는 'roundhouse' 용어를 사용하여 'roundhouse kick'이라고도 합니다.

Expressions
in the opposite direction 반대방향으로
intend to ~하려고 의도하다

먼저 축이 되는 발에 무게중심을 두고, 무릎을 굽혀 바로 몸을 돌립니다.

다음으로 무릎을 펴면서 차는 발을 수평으로 원을 그리게 하여 앞축 또는 발등으로 목표물을 차게 됩니다.

지탱해주는 다리는 발목과 무릎을 곧게 펴서 앞축이 몸의 중심을 잡아주게 합니다.

🎧 `6.4-6.7` 6.4 Trunk Spiral(Turning) Kick

Master   From the Left Hand Forward Stance, the explanation of Trunk Spiral(turning) Kick is as follows;

Looking toward the left foot, one's body turns 180 degrees with one's eye turning 360 degrees to clockwise rotation.

When the body is turned and foot moves together with the Right Forward Stance simultaneously, it is called Half Trunk Spiral(turning) Kick.

If one's body and leg, which is used for kicking, turn 360 degrees completely and the kicked foot is put at the beginning position again, it is called 'Trunk Spiral(turning) Kick'.

Trunk spiral kick

6.5 Dichotomy(Half—Moon) Kick

Master   This is the medium style of the Front Kick and Spiral(turning) Kick.

The fore sole or the foot back delivers a kick by making a slant circle of movement.

6.4 몸돌려차기

사범 왼앞서기 자세에서 몸돌려차기는 다음과 같이 하게 됩니다.

Words

explanation 설명
clockwise 시계방향의
slant 비스듬한

왼발쪽을 보면서 시계방향으로 눈을 360도 돌리면서 몸을 180도 회전합니다.

몸을 돌림과 동시에 발도 오른앞서기로 앞으로 내딛으면 반몸돌려차기가 됩니다.

Expressions

move together 함께
  움직이다

만약 몸과 차기에 사용된 다리가 완전히 360도 회전하고, 차기를 한 발이 제자리에 놓이게 된다면 몸돌려차기가 되는 것입니다.

6.5 반달차기

사범 반달차기는 앞차기와 돌려차기의 중간 형태입니다.

앞축 또는 발등이 비스듬히 원을 그리듯이 차기를 하게 되는 것입니다.

6.6 Twist Kick

Master   If the right foot is kicked from the Left Side Forward Inflection Stance, Twist Kick is executed as follows:

First, the right foot passes the front of body, as the knee is folded and raised as in the Front Kick, toward the left side of the body

And then it abruptly turns toward the right side, finally stretching the knee to deliver a kick.

The applied parts are the fore sole and the foot back.

Here, the body also turns to the left side and then reverses to the right side.

Twist kick

6.7 Back Kick

Master   From the standing position, one lifts the kicking leg and stretches it backward to deliver a kick. The back sole is used for the kick and the ending of the kick is quite similar to the Side Kick.

The foot of the fore leg is used for the kick or that of the back leg can be also applied for the kick

Back kick

6.6 비틀어차기

사범　왼앞굽이에서 오른발로 찬다고 하면 비틀어차기는 다음과 같습니다.

먼저 앞차기에서와 같이 무릎을 접어 올리고, 오른발이 몸 앞쪽을 지나 왼쪽으로 나가게 합니다.

그리고 다시 오른쪽으로 방향을 바꾸어 무릎을 뻗으며 차게 되는 것입니다.

사용부위는 앞축과 발등입니다.

이때 몸도 동시에 왼쪽으로 돌았다가 다시 오른쪽으로 방향을 틀게 됩니다.

6.7 뒤차기

사범　서 있는 자세에서 차고자 하는 다리를 들어 뒤쪽으로 뻗어 차기를 합니다. 뒤축이 차기에 사용되는 부위이며, 차기의 마무리는 옆차기와 비슷합니다.

축이 되는 다리의 발이 차기에 사용되거나 또는 뒷다리를 축이 되는 다리쪽으로 당겨 뒷다리의 발로도 차기를 할 수 있습니다.

Words

abruptly 갑자기, 불쑥
reverse 방향을 뒤집다

Expressions

as follows 다음과 같다
the front of~ ~의 앞에
similar to~ ~와 비슷한

after it is drawn closer to the fore leg.

The former case is applied when the opponent is in the distance while the latter when the opponent is closer to the attacker.

The eyes are directed toward the kicking side and the supporting leg may not stretch the knee and the ankle as in the Side Kick.

The upper part of the body leans more forward than in the side kick.

 ## 6.8 Stretch Kick

Master This is similar to the Front Kick but the knee of kicking leg does not fold too much.

The foot is simply lifted up in the right front to deliver a kick by stretching.

Unlike the Front Kick, the foot does not face upward, but simply moves forward by the stretch of leg to counter the opponent's advance. The kick mainly targets below the trunk.

Stretch kick

전자(앞다리 사용)는 상대방이 멀리 있을 때에 사용되며, 반면에 후자
(뒷다리 사용)는 상대방이 가까이 있을 때 사용합니다.

Words

the former case 전자
the latter 후자
lean 기대다
counter 대응하다, 맞
　받아치다

눈은 차기를 하는 쪽을 향하며, 받쳐주는 다리는 옆차기에서와 같이
무릎과 발목을 펴지 않아도 됩니다.

몸의 상체부위는 옆차기보다 조금 더 앞으로 기울이면 됩니다.

6.8 뻗어차기

Expressions

opponent's advance
상대방의 접근(전진)

사범　뻗어차기는 앞차기와 비슷하지만, 차는 다리의 무릎을 많이 접을 필
요는 없습니다.

발을 가볍게 오른쪽으로 들어올려 뻗으면서 차기를 하면 됩니다.

앞차기와는 달리 발이 위로 향하지 않고, 상대방의 접근에 대응하기
위해 발을 뻗으면서 앞으로 약간 움직이면 됩니다. 차기는 주로 몸통
아래를 목표로 하는 것이죠.

Push kick

6.9 Push Kick

Master The way of kicking is the same as the Side Kick or the stretch kick but the kicking is slowed down, merely pushing the target instead of inflicting a blow.

This is used especially when the target is nearer. Instead of inflicting a vital damage, this technique is intended to throw down or push away the opponent.

The sole of the foot is used for the kick.

6.10 Hook Kick

Hook kick

Master When the opponent has evaded the kick on the moment of delivering a kick attack and comes closer to the attacker, the kicking leg, which has missed and passed the target will attack the back of the opponent's head or the back by the force of folding the stretched knee.

If Spiral(turning) Kick has missed the target, the kicking leg will instantly fold the knee, delivering a kick by the heel.

6.9 밀어차기

사범 차는 방법은 옆차기나 뻗어차기와 비슷하지만, 단지 목표물에 타격을 가하기보다는 밀면서 약간 느리게 차는 것입니다.

Words
merely 그저, 단지
especially 특히
vital damage 큰 상처
evade 피하다
instantly 즉시, 즉각

이 기술은 목표물이 아주 가까이 있을 때 사용됩니다. 어떤 큰 상처를 입히기 보다는 넘어뜨리거나 멀리 떨어지게 하기 위함인 것이죠.

발의 축이 차기에 사용됩니다.

Expressions
instead of~ ~ 대신에
intend to~ ~하려고
　　　의도하다

6.10 낚아차기

사범 상대방이 공격하는 사람의 차기를 피해 접근하는 경우, 상대를 놓치고 지나쳐버린 발로 뻗은 무릎을 굽히는 힘으로 상대방의 머리 뒤 또는 등을 공격하는 것입니다.

만약 돌려차기로 목표물을 놓친 경우라면 차기를 한 발의 무릎을 잽싸게 굽혀 뒤꿈치로 차기를 하면 됩니다.

6.11 Thrash Kick

Master The kicking leg will be lifted high up above the opponent's head and inflict a kick, bringing down the leg with the knee keeping stretched.

The heel and the sole are used for this kick.

6.12 Inner Kick

Master Just like the Dichotomy(Semilunar) Kick, this kick is executed by making the kicking foot draw a circle from outside to inside.

Inner kick

The back of the foot blade is used for this technique, which is applied on the moment of lifting up the foot before Downward Kick or in the course of the Target Kick.

 6.13-6.17 ### 6.13 Outer Kick

Master This is the opposite way of Front Kick and similar to the Twist Kick, using the back of the foot. It is mainly used in defense technique.

Outer kick

6.14 Hold Kick

Master It is sometimes necessary to hold the opponent by the

6.11 내려차기

사범 차기를 하는 발을 상대방 머리 위로 높이 들어 무릎을 뻗은 채로 다리를 내리며 가격하는 기술입니다.

뒤꿈치와 축이 내려차기에 사용되는 부위입니다.

6.12 안차기

사범 반달차기의 경우와 같이 안차기는 차는 발이 바깥에서 안으로 원을 그리며 차는 것입니다.

발날등부위가 이 기술에 사용되며, 내려차기 또는 표적차기 전에 발을 올리는 순간에 적용되는 것입니다.

6.13 바깥차기

사범 바깥차기는 안차기의 반대이며 비틀어차기와 비슷한데요, 발등을 사용하는 것입니다. 주로 막기 기술에 사용됩니다.

6.14 잡고차기

사범 때때로 차기 전에 상대방을 도복이나 신체 일부로 잡을 필요가 있습

Words

dichotomy 이분의, 양분의
necessary 필요한

Expressions

keep stretched 뻗은 상태를 유지하다
draw a circle 원을 그리다
from outside to inside 밖에서 안쪽으로
similar to~ ~와 유사한

Hold kick

uniform or the bodily parts before delivering a kick.

This way attempts to bear down the opponent, thus doubling the effect of the blow.

6.15 Rolling Kick

Master Mainly from the Backward Inflection Stance, one raises the fore foot, and makes it rolled on the ground, moving the body forward by the impellent force.

And as soon as the back foot follows the fore foot, landing on the ground, he or she makes the fore foot deliver a kick.

This technique is intended to deceive the opponent pretending to attack at the first movement but the attack comes a moment later.

6.16 Jump Kick

Master This is a technique of kicking by one foot while the body jumps up in the air.

It is possible to perform this technique from the Close Stance, but in general it can be better

Jump kick

니다.

이 방식은 상대방을 압도하여 가격하는 효과를 배가시키기 위함입니다.

6.15 굴러차기

사범 주로 뒷굽이 자세에서 앞발을 들어 바닥을 구르듯이 찬 후에 추진력으로 몸을 앞으로 나아갑니다.

그리고 뒷발이 앞발에 따라 붙었을 때 바닥으로 내딛으면서 앞발로 차기를 하는 것입니다.

이 기술은 상대방을 첫 움직임에 공격하는 것처럼 속이기 위함이며, 실제로는 나중에 공격하는 것이죠.

6.16 뛰어차기

사범 뛰어차기는 몸을 공중에 띄운 채로 한쪽 발로 차기를 하는 기술입니다.

이 기술은 모아서기에서 할 수도 있으나, 일반적으로 두 발이 넓게 벌려 있는 뒷굽이에서 하는 것이 더 좋습니다.

Words
uniform 도복
double 배가하다
impellent force 추진
  력
pretend ~인 척하다

Expressions
attempt to 시도하다
in the air 공중에서

carried out from the Backward Inflection Stance, in which the two feet are wide apart.

In detail, the two feet push the ground simultaneously to jump up in the air.

Either the fore foot or back foot alone can push the ground to lift the body in the air.

6.17 Two Feet Alternate Kick

Master   After the body jumps up in the air, two feet perform kicks alternately.

The back-foot kicks first and the fore foot later.

The first kick is in the disguise or aims at a lower part, and the later kick must kick the target accurately and higher.

The Two Feet Alternate Kick can be performed either by advancing forward to reach the distanced opponent or by jumping up higher to reach a high target.

Two Feet Alternate kick

부연하면, 두 발로 동시에 바닥을 차서 공중으로 뛰어오를 수 있기 때문입니다.

앞발 또는 뒷발 하나만으로도 바닥을 차고 내딛어 공중에 몸을 띄울 수도 있습니다.

6.17 두발당성차기

사범 몸을 공중에 띄운 후에 두 발로 차기를 번갈아가며 하는 것입니다.

뒷발로 먼저 차고, 나중에 앞발로 차기를 합니다.

첫 번째 차기는 속이듯이 하거나 아래 부위를 목표로 하며, 이어지는 차기는 정확하고 높게 하여 반드시 공격 목표를 대상으로 해야 합니다.

두발당성차기는 원거리에 있는 상대방에게 앞으로 다가가거나 또는 높은 곳에 있는 목표물에 높게 뛰어서 수행하게 됩니다.

Words
alternately 번갈아서
accurately 정확하게

Expressions
wide apart 넓게 벌린 채
in detail 부연하면
in the disguise 속이는 듯하게

Combined feet kick

 6.18-6.22 ## 6.18 Combined(Joint) Feet Kick

Master   Jumping up in the air, one joins the two feet close and make them kick the same target at a time.

When jumping up, the two feet are drawn closer to push up the body.

6.19 Scissors Kick

Master   Scissors Kick, as a fantastic type with its advanced technique, can often be seen at football games.

As in the Combined(Joint) Feet Kick, the two feet kick two targets at a time by separating the feet from each other.

6.20 Repeated Kick

Repeated kick

Master   One leg performs more than two kicks in the same manner.

Generally, the first kick aims at underneath targets while the second at the trunk or the face.

However, Repeated Kick can be directed to the same target.

6.18 모둠차기

사범 공중에 뜬 채로 두 발을 가깝게 모으고, 모은 두 발로 하나의 목표물을 동시에 차게 됩니다.

띌 때에는 두 발을 가깝게 하여 몸을 밀어줍니다.

6.19 가위차기

사범 가위차기는 축구에서도 가끔 볼 수 있는 고난도의 멋진 차기 형태입니다.

모듬차기에서와 같이 두 발이 서로 순서대로 두 개의 목표물을 동시에 차게 됩니다.

6.20 거듭차기

사범 한 다리로 2회 이상의 차기를 같은 방식으로 수행하는 것입니다.

일반적으로 첫 번째 차기는 아래 목표를 겨냥하고, 두 번째 차기는 몸통이나 얼굴을 목표로 합니다.

그러나 거듭차기는 동일한 목표를 향해서 수행할 수도 있습니다.

Words

join ~에 참여하다
fantastic 고난도의, 멋진
separate 나누다

Expressions

at a time 동시에
in the same manner 같은 방법으로
directed to~ ~를 향하다

The first kick is largely intended to deceive the opponent and the second one must be perfect to overpower him or her.

The Repeated Kick is also broken down into three types: (a) Repeated Front Kick, (b) Repeated Side Kick, (c) Repeated Spiral(Turning) Kick

6.21 Mixed Kick

Master   Mixed Kick uses more than two kick techniques by one foot.

One might think that the foot falls down to the ground at the time of delivering the second kick.

But without touching the ground, one changes the direction and applies the second kick technique.

In order to get closer to the opponent, the supporting foot slips deep toward him or her at the same time that the second kick is delivered.

Of course, the kicking foot may touch the ground lightly in order to accelerate the impellent force before carrying out the second kick, rushing into the opponent.

첫 번째 차기는 대개 상대방을 속이기 위한 것이고, 두 번째 차기는 그 상대방을 완전히 제압할 수 있어야 합니다.

거듭차기는 또한 (a) 거듭앞차기, (b) 거듭옆차기, (c) 거듭돌려차기의 세 가지 동작으로 나누어집니다.

Words
deceive 속이다, 기만하다
overpower 제압하다, 압도하다
accelerate 가속하다
impellent force 추진력

6.21 섞어차기

사범 섞어차기는 한 발로 두 가지 이상의 차기 기술을 사용하는 것입니다.

일반적으로 두 번째 차기를 하기 전에 발이 땅에 닿는 것이라고 생각할지도 모르겠습니다.

Expressions
intend to~ ~하려고 의도하다
in order to~ ~하기 위하여

그러나 땅에 닿지 않고, 방향을 바꿔 두 번째 차기 기술을 사용하는 것입니다.

상대방에 가까이 다가가기 위해서는 두 번째 차기를 하는 순간에 허공에 있지 않은 다른 디딤발이 동시에 상대방에게 미끄러지듯 밀착하게 해야 합니다.

때때로 두 번째 차기를 하기 전에 가속도를 붙이며, 상대방에게 빠르게 돌진하기 위해서 첫 번째 차기를 한 발이 땅에 약간 닿을 수도 있습니다.

Types of Mixed Kicks are (a) Fronk Kick and Spiral(Turning) Kick, (b) Front Kick and Side Kick, (c) Twist Kick and Spiral(Turning) Kick

6.22 Successive Kick

Master The same kick techniques is applied alternately by left and right foot.

 6.23 Successive Mixed Kick

Master Left and right foot deliver kicks alternately (in turn).

Meanwhile, not like the Successive Kick, the different kick techniques are applied.

6.24 Jump Successive Kick

Master While keeping the body in the air after jumping, one executes the same kick technique alternately (in turn).

6.25 Jump Over Kick

Master Jumping over the obstacle, one delivers the kick technique.

Jump over kick

섞어차기에는 몇 가지 종류가 있습니다 : (a) 앞차고돌려차기, (b) 앞차고옆차기, (c) 비틀어차기하고돌려차기

Words

successive 연속적인
alternately 번갈아서
meanwhile 그런데
obstacle 장애물

6.22 이어차기

사범 왼발과 오른발을 번갈아 사용하여 차기를 하는 기술입니다.

6.23 이어섞어차기

사범 왼발과 오른발로 번갈아가며 차기를 수행합니다.

Expressions

in turn 차례로
in the air 공중에서

그런데 이어차기와는 다르게 각각 다른 차기 기술을 수행하는 것을 말합니다.

6.24 뛰어이어차기

사범 뛰고 난 후 몸을 공중에 띄운 상태에서 양 발을 번갈아가며 차기 기술을 수행하는 것입니다.

6.25 뛰어넘어차기

사범 장애물을 건너뛰면서 차기 기술을 구사하는 것입니다.

The jump over kick technique is divided into two contrary types. First one is the high jump over short kicking.

On the contrary, the long jump over distanced kicking is the second type.

The height of the above second type will not be so much due to its relevant distanced kick.

6.26 Single Line Kick

Single line kick

Master Pushing up the body in the air, one opens the feet left and right on a single line toward each target and delivers simultaneous kicks.

Usually both the Side Kick and Twist Kick are applied concurrently. Some call this technique as scissors kick but it is not correct.

There are two types of Single Line Kick.

The one is Horizontal Single Line Kick and applied when the two targets are horizontally placed.

The other is Different Height Single Line Kick and applicable when the two targets are placed with

이 기술은 두 가지 상반된 유형이 있습니다. 첫 번째 유형은 높이 뛰며 짧게 끊어 차기를 하는 것입니다.

반면에 먼 거리로 차면서 멀리 뛰는 것은 두 번째 유형입니다.

두 번째 유형은 먼 거리로 차기 때문에 당연히 낮게 점프하게 될 것입니다.

6.26 일자차기

사범 몸을 공중에 뛰어 올리면서 두 발이 일자가 되도록 좌우로 펼치듯이 벌려 각각의 목표물을 동시에 차는 것입니다.

대개 옆차기와 비틀어차기가 동시에 이루어집니다. 어떤 사람은 이 기술을 가위차기라고 하는데, 그것은 맞지 않는 말입니다.

일자차기에는 두 종류가 있습니다.

첫 번째는 수평일자차기인데요. 두 개의 목표물이 동일선상에 수평으로 있을 때 사용됩니다.

다른 하나는 비켜일자차기인데요. 두 개의 목표물이 서로 다른 높이에 있을 때 사용됩니다.

Words

contrary 상반된, 반대의
relevant 적절한
concurrently 동시에
scissor 가위
horizontally 수평으로

Expressions

divided into ~로 나누어진
on the contrary 반대로
on a single line 일자가 되도록

different heights from each other.

6.27 Multi Direction Kick

Master While the body is kept in the air, one kicks multiple targets.

Foot techniques are numerous, so this is called the Multi Direction Kick.

Applicable actions are both foot techniques and hand techniques.

6.28 Single Mountain Shape Side Kick

Single mountain shape side kick

Master While the arms make Single Mountain Shape Blocking, Side Kick is delivered at the same time.

Defending the punch attack from the rear by the Outer Blocking, one delivers Side Kick simultaneously, which is accompanied also by the punch of the other hand.

6.29 Target Kick

Target kick

Master By setting an imaginary target in the palm, one practices the inner kick by the back of foot blade.

6.27 다방향차기

사범 몸이 공중에 뜬 채로 여러 개의 목표물을 차는 것입니다.

발기술은 매우 가짓수가 많습니다. 그래서 이 기술은 다방향차기라고 부릅니다.

발기술과 손기술을 모두 사용할 수 있습니다.

6.28 외산틀옆차기

사범 외산틀옆차기는 양팔로 외산틀막기를 하면서 동시에 옆차기를 하는 것입니다.

바깥막기로 상대방이 뒤에서 하는 지르기 공격을 방어하면서, 동시에 다른 손으로 지르기를 하고 옆차기하는 것입니다.

6.29 표적차기

사범 손바닥으로 가상의 목표물을 정해서 가늠한 다음 발날등으로 안차기 하는 것입니다.

Words

multiple 여러 개의
defend 방어하다
imaginary 상상의

Expressions

at the same time 동시
에
from the rear 뒤쪽으
로부터
be accompanied by
~을 함께하다

7. Grasp

Master Until now, we have learned six major movements. Great job.

Next, some more movements will not have many detailed types so I hope you could learn faster. Please put forth some more of your energies.

The Grasp, together with Blocking, is one of the important defense techniques.

7.1 Arc Hand Wrist Grasp

Arc hand wrist grasp

Master An arc-hand is used to grab the opponent's wrist in the course of the latter's downward hit.

Disciple Master, the word 'arc hand' is quite new to me. Would you give us more details?

Master Sure, arc hand is shaped by widening the thumb and index fingers. This is mainly used to attack the opponent's uvula or neck.

Disciple It could be a stronger weapon than I thought. Thanks for the explanation.

7. 잡기

사범	지금까지 여섯 가지 주요 동작을 배워보았는데요, 모두 수고했습니다.

Words
important 중요한
uvula 목젖
weapon 무기

다음으로 배워나갈 동작들은 세부 유형이 많지 않아 빨리 나아갈 수 있으리라 생각하니, 조금만 더 힘을 내기 바랍니다.

잡기는 막기와 함께 중요한 방어 동작의 한 가지입니다.

Expressions
until now 지금부터
put forth 내어놓다, 제한하다

7.1 아금손팔목잡기

사범 상대방이 내려치기를 하는 순간에 상대방의 팔목을 아금손으로 잡습니다.

문하생 사범님, 그런데 '아금손'이라는 용어는 처음 들어보는데요. 조금 더 설명해 주시겠습니까?

사범 물론입니다. 아금손은 엄지손가락과 검지(집게)손가락을 벌려서 V자형으로 만드는 것입니다. 주로 상대의 목젖이나 턱을 가격할 때 쓰입니다.

문하생 생각보다 강력한 무기가 될 수도 있겠네요. 잘 알겠습니다.

Wrist grasp

Wrist twist grasp & pulling

Ankle/head/shoulder
grasp

Neck grasp

7.2 Wrist Grasp

Master Wrist Grasp is mostly used in Poomsae 'Chonkwon'.

7.3 Wrist Twist Grasp & Pulling

Master After acting the hand-blade twist-blocking of the trunk, the wrist is slowly turned toward the hand-blade to twist and drag in.

7.4 Ankle/Head/Shoulder Grasp

Master According to the opponent's bodily parts to grasp, there are Ankle Grasp, Head Grasp, and Shoulder Grasp.

7.5 Neck Grasp

Master A pincers-hand is used to grasp the opponent's neck.

7.2 팔목잡기

사범 팔목잡기는 품새 '천권'에서 주로 사용됩니다.

Words

mostly 주로
slowly 천천히
grasp 잡다, 움켜쥐다

7.3 팔목비틀어잡아끌기

사범 손날비틀어몸통막기를 한 후에 팔목을 천천히 손날쪽으로 돌려 틀어 잡고 끌어당깁니다.

Expressions

drag in 끌어당기다
according to~ ~에 따라

7.4 발목잡기

사범 잡는 부위에 따라 각각 발목/머리/어깨잡기가 있습니다.

7.5 목잡기

사범 상대방의 목을 집게손으로 잡습니다.

8. Breaking

Master   Breaking is one of the attack(offense) techniques.

This is to immobilize the opponent by pushing or twisting the joint parts.

Disciple When could it be effectively used?

Master   Oh, I was going to talk about it. Your question is quite well-timed.

It is mainly used when capturing the opponent or being captured by her or him in a close distance.

8.1 Wrist Breaking

Wrist breaking

Master   By using hand, this technique overpowers the opponent by pushing or twisting her or his wrist.

8.2 Elbow Breaking

Elbow breaking

Master   Like the Wrist Breaking, this technique suppresses the opponent by pushing or twisting her or his elbow.

8. 꺾기

사범   꺾기는 공격 기술의 한 가지입니다.

상대방의 관절을 누르거나 비틀어서 움직이지 못하게 하는 기술입니다.

문하생   이건 주로 언제 사용하면 좋은가요?

사범   네, 이어서 말해주려 했는데요. 먼저 질문 잘해주었습니다.

가까운 거리에서 상대방에게 잡혔을 때나 상대방을 잡았을 때 활용합니다.

8.1 팔목꺾기

사범   손으로 상대방의 팔목을 누르거나 비틀어서 제압하는 기술입니다.

8.2 팔굽꺾기

사범   팔목꺾기와 마찬가지로 이 기술은 손으로 상대방의 팔굽을 누르거나 비틀어서 제압하는 기술입니다.

Words

immobilize 움직이지
  못하게 하다
effectively 효과적으로
capture 붙잡다
well-timed 시기적절한
overpower 제압하다,
  압도하다
suppress 누르다

Expressions

in a close distance 가
까운 거리에서

Knee breaking

8.3 Knee Breaking

Master One hand grabs foot back pivot, the other arc hand attacks the opponent's knee.

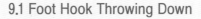

9. Throwing Down

Master Throwing down is one of the offense techniques.

This is to throw down the opponent after making him or her lose balance by pulling or pushing,

Foot hook throwing down

9.1 Foot Hook Throwing Down

Master This action trips up with the opponent's foot.

Foot lift-up throwing down

9.2 Foot Lift-Up Throwing Down

Master This action lifts up the foot and makes the opponent fall down.

8.3 무릎꺾기

사범 한 손으로 발목을 잡고, 다른 아금손으로 상대방의 무릎을 공격합니다.

Words

knee 무릎
pull 당기다
push 밀다

9. 넘기기

사범 넘기기는 공격 기술의 한 종류입니다.

상대방을 잡아당기거나 밀치며 중심을 무너뜨린 다음 쓰러뜨리는 기술입니다.

Expressions

throw down 넘기다
lose balance 균형을
    잃게하다
lift up 들어올리다

9.1 발걸어넘기기

사범 발을 걸어 넘기는 동작입니다.

9.2 발들어넘기기

사범 발을 들어 상대를 넘어뜨리는 동작입니다.

10. Special Poom

Master   Today, we will exercise Special Poom. The term 'Special Poom' might be also unique and unfamiliar to you.

Disciple I'm not sure but I once heard that it is preparatory motion for proceeding into the next technique.

Master   Correct. To add more, it executes both attack and defense techniques simultaneously and/or imitates the image of an object with special posture.

Special Poom covers three areas of actions, preparatory Poom to perform actions, and physical functions.

As I mentioned just before, actions have capacities of both attack and defense techniques.

Preparatory Poom refers to those preparatory postures just ahead to performing attack and defense techniques.

Also, capacities of physical functions aim to develop muscular strength and to increase movable range.

10. 특수품

사범 오늘은 특수품에 대해 배워보겠습니다. 특수품이란 용어도 특이하고 생소하죠?

문하생 정확하진 않지만, 다음 기술을 하기 위한 예비동작이라고 들은 것 같습니다.

사범 맞습니다. 덧붙이자면, 공격과 방어 기술을 동시에 하거나 사물의 모습 등을 모방한 특수한 자세입니다.

특수품이 내포하는 세 가지 부분은 동작, 동작을 수행하기 위한 예비품, 그리고 체육적 기능입니다.

조금 전에 말씀드렸듯이 동작은 공격과 방어 기술을 수행할 수 있게 하는 것입니다.

예비품은 위의 공격과 방어 기술을 수행하기 위한 예비 자세라고 할 수 있습니다.

또한 체육적 기능은 근력 향상 및 가동범위의 확대를 가능하게 합니다.

Words

unique 특이한
unfamiliar 생소한, 익숙하지 않은
preparatory 예비의
proceed 진행하다
imitate 모방하다, 흉내내다
posture 자세
mention 말하다, 언급하다
capacity 능력, 용량
muscular strength 근력
movable range 가동범위

Expressions

refer to~ ~을 나타내다, ~와 관련 있다
aim to~ ~을 목표로 하다

All the above Pooms are called 'Special Poom'.

10.1 Bigger Hinge

Bigger hinge

Master   Bigger Hinge is used as attack(offense), defense, and preparation action.

The hand on the waist keeps its base part facing upward.

The fist crossing the solar plexus line forms the shape of a turned-over fist.

At this moment, the arm laid in front of the solar plexus keeps itself slightly aloof from the trunk

10.2 Smaller Hinge

Smaller hinge

Master   The hand on the waist keeps its base part facing upward.

Hammer-Fist is piled up right over the top of the other fist.

There is a small gap between the two fists.

위의 모든 품을 특수품이라고 합니다.

10.1 큰돌쩌귀

Words
Bigger Hinge 큰돌쩌귀
preparation 준비

사범 큰돌쩌귀는 공격, 방어, 예비동작으로 사용됩니다.

허리에 있는 손은 손바닥부분이 위를 향하게 합니다.

명치선상을 가로지른 주먹은 엎은 주먹 형태가 되게 합니다.

Expressions
keep aloof from~ ~
   와 간격을 두다
pile up 포개어올리다

이때 명치앞에 놓인 팔은 몸통과 약간 간격을 둡니다.

10.2 작은돌쩌귀

사범 허리에 있는 손은 손바닥부분이 위를 향하게 합니다.

다른 주먹의 바로 위에 메주먹을 포개어 놓습니다.

두 주먹의 사이는 약간 간격을 둡니다.

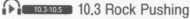 **10.3 Rock Pushing**

Rock pushing

Master   In a forward inflection stance, two hands are stuck to one side of the waist.

The hand on the side of the rear foot comes downward and the one on the side of the fore foot goes upward respectively, keeping themselves unfolded and their base parts directed toward the front side.

The two hands are pushed up diagonally to be placed in front of the face(forehead).

And the finger-tips of both hands are directed upward from the diagonal line.

10.4 Mountain Pushing

Mountain pushing

Master   In Tiger Stance, the Palm Hand is placed in front of the chest, keeping the finger-tips on the fore-foot side below and those on the rear-foot side above.

The Palm Hands are simultaneously pushed forward, making the upper hand stop its movement in front of the philtrum with its elbow straightly unfolded.

10.3 바위밀기

사범 앞굽이 자세에서 두 손을 한쪽 허리로 갖다 붙입니다.

뒷발쪽에 있는 손을 아래로 하고, 앞발쪽의 손은 위로 하여 손을 펴서 손바닥부분이 앞쪽을 향하게 합니다.

두 손을 대각선 형태로 올려 밀어서 얼굴(이마) 앞쪽에 위치하도록 합니다.

그리고 양 손끝이 대각선에서 위로 향하게 하면 됩니다.

10.4 태산밀기

사범 범서기에서 앞발쪽의 손끝은 아래로 하고, 뒷발쪽의 손끝은 위로 하여 바탕손을 가슴 앞쪽에 위치시킵니다.

바탕손을 동시에 앞쪽으로 밀어 윗손은 팔굽을 곧게 편 상태에서 인중 앞에 멈추게 합니다.

Words

rear foot 뒷발
philtrum 인중
respectively 각자, 제
  각각
diagonally 대각선으로

Expressions

stick to ~에 고정하다
in front of~ ~의 앞에

And the lower hand stops its movement in front of the lower abdomen with its elbow unfolded.

10.5 Wing Spreading

Wing spreading

Master   From the overlapped hands in Close Stance, the hands are pulled up to the front of the chest.

Two hands are opened apart from each other so that the palms may look like pushing outward respectively to the sides of the shoulders.

And finger-tips are kept facing upward and the elbow straightly unfolded sideward.

그리고 아랫손은 팔굽을 편 상태에서 복부 아래의 앞에서 멈추게 하면 됩니다.

10.5 날개펴기

Words

lower abdomen 아랫배
overlap 겹치다
straightly 곧게

사범 모아서기에서 겹손으로 손을 가슴앞까지 끌어올립니다.

두 손을 옆으로 벌려서 손바닥이 양쪽 어깨의 옆을 각각 미는 것처럼 보이게 합니다.

그리고 손끝이 위를 향하게 하고, 팔굽을 옆으로 곧게 펴면 됩니다.

Expressions

pull up to~ ~까지 끌
 어올리다
look like ~처럼 보이다

Part 3
Poomsae

품새

Master   We've learn about several basic movements so far and will move to next part 'Poomsae'.

Disciple   Would you briefly explain about Poomsae and Poom? We've heard about it from time to time but still do not know the accurate meaning.

Master   I see. It's quite simple.

Each Poom of the Poomsae has been inherited through a long history of about 5,000 years, finally as a product of scientific technique formulated based on the traditional national spirit and practical experiments.

From the technical viewpoint, the Poomsae itself is Taekwondo, and the basic movements are no more than the preliminary actions to reach the Poomsae.

The Kyorugi is a practical application of the Poomsae and the Taekwondo spirit is manifested not in an abstract mental philosophy expressed in the documents but in the actions of poomsae.

Disciple   Then, what is the Taekwondo Poomsae?

사범   지금까지 여러 기본동작을 배워보았는데요, 이제 품새로 넘어가겠습니다.

문하생 '품새'나 '품'에 대해 간단히 설명해주시겠습니까? 자주 들어왔지만 정확한 의미는 아직 모르거든요.

Words

briefly 간단히
accurate 정확한
inherite 물려받다, 상속받다
scientific 과학적인
formulate 쌓이다
traditional 전통적인
experiment 실험
viewpoint 관점
preliminary 예비의
manifest 나타내다
abstract 추상적인

사범   네, 알겠습니다. 사실 간단하고 쉬운 것입니다.

품새의 각 품은 약 5,000년 동안의 긴 역사를 통해 유래가 된 것인데요, 전통 국가정신과 실전경험을 토대로 하여 쌓여온 과학적 기술의 산물이라 할 수 있습니다.

Expressions

from time to time 가끔, 이따금
no more than~ 단지 ~에 지나지 않다

기술적 관점에서 보면 품새 자체는 태권도이며, 기본동작들은 품새를 하기 위한 예비행동에 지나지 않는 것이죠.

겨루기는 품새의 실전적 응용이며, 태권도 정신은 문서로 전해온 추상적인 정신철학이 아닌 품새의 행위로 나타나는 것입니다.

문하생 그렇다면 태권도 품새란 무엇일까요?

Master   The Poomsae is the style of conduct which expresses directly or indirectly mental and physical refinements as well as the principles of attack(offense) and defense resulting from cultivation of Taekwondo spirit and techniques.

Poomsae consists of Taegeuk 1 Jang to 8 Jang and are classified as Kup grader's poomsaes.

And the Poomsaes from Koryo up to Ilyo are classified for Dan-grader's.

The Poomsae consists of basic movements and Poom and they are so arranged to fit the frame of movement direction, which is called the Poomsae line.

The Poomsae lines are described after symbols or Chinese characters.

1. Taegeuk 1~8 Jang for Kup Graders

 1.1 Taegeuk 1 Jang

Master   Taegeuk 1 Jang represents the symbol of 'Keon' which is one of the 8 Kwaes and 'Keon' means the heaven and 'Yang'.

사범   품새란 태권도 정신과 기술의 정수를 직접적 또는 간접적으로 나타
낸 행동양식이며, 태권도 정신과 기술의 수양을 통해 공격과 방어의
원리를 표현하는 것입니다.

Words

directly 직접적으로
indirectly 간접적으로
refinement 개선
principle 원칙
cultivation 함양, 경작,
재배
represent 대표하다

품새는 태극 1장부터 8장까지로 되어 있으며, 이것은 유급자를 위한
품새로 분류된 것입니다.

그리고 고려부터 일여까지의 품새들은 유단자를 위한 것입니다.

품새는 기본동작과 품으로 구성되어 있는데요, 품새선이라 불리는 운
동방향의 틀에 맞추게 되어 있습니다.

Expressions

result from~ ~이 원
인이다
consists of~ ~로 구성
되다
classified as~ ~로 분
류되다

품새선은 기호와 중국 문자로 설명되어 있습니다.

1. 유급자를 위한 태극 1~8장

1.1 태극 1장

사범   태극 1장은 팔괘의 '건'을 의미하며, '건'은 하늘과 '양'을 뜻합니다.

As the 'Keon' symbolizes the beginnings of all creatures, so does the Taegeuk 1 Jang in the training of Taekwondo.

Movements and turns of Poomsae Taegeuk 1 Jang are as follows;

First, at ready position, Basic Ready Stance looking toward bottom.

[1] Toward top–right direction, putting forth left foot to step down, Left Side Forward Stance and Low Blocking

[2] Toward top–right direction, putting forth right foot to step down, Right Side Forward Stance and Trunk Opposite Punch

[3] Toward top–left, putting forth right foot to step down, Right Side Forward Stance and Low Blocking

'건'이 만물의 근원을 나타내는 것과 같이, 태권도에서도 가장 처음 시작하는 품새입니다.

Words

symbolize 상징하다
beginning 근원, 시작
creature 창조물, 만물
direction 방향

태극 1장의 동작과 순서는 다음과 같습니다.

처음에 준비 위치에서 아래 방향을 보며 기본준비서기

[1] 오른쪽 위 방향으로 왼발을 내디디며 왼앞서기 내려막기

[2] 오른쪽 위 방향으로 오른발을 내디디며 오른앞서기 몸통반대지르기

[3] 왼쪽 위 방향으로 오른발을 내디뎌 오른앞서기 내려막기

[4] Toward top−left direction, putting forth left foot to step down, Left Side Forward Stance and Trunk Opposite Punch

[5] Toward bottom, moving left foot to turn around, Left Side Forward Inflection Stance and Low Blocking

[6] Toward bottom, putting two feet at their places, Left Side Forward Inflection Stance and Trunk Right(Straight) Punch

[7] Toward middle−left, moving right foot to step down, Right Side Forward Stance and Trunk Inner Blocking

[8] Toward middle−left, putting forth left foot to step down, Left Side Forward Inflection Stance and Trunk Right(Straight) Punch

[4] 왼쪽 위 방향으로 왼발을 내디디며 왼앞서기 몸통반대지르기

Words

opposite 반대의
inflection 굽이, 굴절
bottom 바닥, 아래쪽

[5] 아래 방향으로 왼발 옮겨 돌아서 왼앞굽이 내려막기

[6] 아래 방향으로 두 발 제자리에 두고 왼앞굽이 몸통바로지르기

[7] 왼쪽 중간 방향으로 오른발을 옮겨 딛고 오른앞서기 몸통안막기

[8] 왼쪽 중간 방향으로 왼발 내디뎌 왼앞서기 몸통바로지르기

[9] Toward middle—right, moving left foot to step down, Left Side Forward Stance and Trunk Inner Blocking

[10] Toward middle—right, putting forth right foot to step down, Right Side Forward Inflection Stance and Trunk Right(Straight) Punch

 1.2 Taegeuk 2 Jang

Master   Taegeuk 2 Jang symbolizes the 'Tae' which is one of the 8 divination signs. 'Tae' signifies both the inner firmness and the outer softness.

Movements and turns of Poomsae Taegeuk 2 Jang are as follows;

At ready position, Basic Ready Stance looking toward bottom.

[1] Toward top—right, putting forth left foot to step down, Left Side Forward Stance and Low Blocking

[9] 오른쪽 중간 방향으로 왼발 옮겨 뒤로 돌아서 왼앞서기 몸통안막기

[10] 오른쪽 중간 방향으로 오른발 내디뎌 오른앞서기 몸통바로지르기

Words

inflection 굽이
symbolize 상징하다,
  의미하다
8 divination signs 8괘
signify 의미하다, 뜻
  하다
firmness 단단함
softness 부드러움

1.2 태극 2장

태극 2장은 팔괘의 '태'를 의미하며, '태'는 속으로 단단하고 겉으로는 부드럽다는 뜻입니다.

태극 2장의 동작과 순서는 다음과 같습니다.

준비 위치에서 아래 방향을 보며 기본준비서기

[1] 오른쪽 위 방향으로 왼발 내디뎌 왼앞서기 내려막기

[2] Toward top-right direction, putting forth right foot to step down, Right Side Forward Inflection Stance and Trunk Opposite Punch

[3] Toward top-left, moving back right foot to turn around, Right Side Forward Stance and Low Blocking

[4] Toward top-left, putting forth left foot to step down, Left Side Forward Inflection Stance and Trunk Opposite Punch

[5] Toward bottom, moving left foot to turn around, Left Side Forward Stance and Trunk Inner Blocking

[6] Toward bottom, putting forth right foot to step down, Right Side Forward Stance and Trunk Inner Blocking

[2] 오른쪽 위 방향으로 오른발을 내디디며 오른앞굽이 몸통반대지르기

Words

opposite 반대의
bottom 아래, 바닥

[3] 왼쪽 위 방향으로 오른발 옮겨 뒤로 돌아서 오른앞서기 내려막기

[4] 왼쪽 위 방향으로 왼발 내디뎌 왼앞굽이 몸통반대지르기

Expressions

turn around 돌다

[5] 아래 방향으로 왼발 옮겨 돌아서 왼앞서기 몸통안막기

[6] 아래 방향으로 오른발을 내디디며 오른앞서기 몸통안막기

[7] Toward middle−right, moving left foot to step down, Left Side Forward Stance and Low Blocking

[8] Toward middle−right, Right Foot Forward Kick to step down. Next, Right Side Forward Inflection Stance and Face Opposite Punch

[9] Toward middle−left, moving back right foot to turn around, Right Side Forward Stance and Low Blocking

[10] Toward middle−left, Left Foot Forward Kick to step down. Next, Left Side Forward Inflection Stance and Face Opposite Punch

 1.3 Taegeuk 3 Jang

Master   Taegeuk 3 Jang symbolizes the 'Ree' which is one of the 8 divination signs. 'Ree' represents fire and

[7] 오른쪽 중간 방향으로 왼발 옮겨 디뎌 왼앞서기 내려막기

Words

symbolize 상징하다
represent 나타내다

[8] 오른쪽 중간 방향으로 오른발 앞차기 하고 내디뎌 오른앞굽이 얼굴반대지르기

[9] 왼쪽 중간 방향으로 오른발 옮겨 뒤로 돌아서 오른앞서기 내려막기

[10] 왼쪽 중간 방향으로 왼발 앞차기 하고 내디뎌 왼앞굽이 얼굴반대지르기

1.3 태극 3장

사범   태극 3장은 팔괘의 '이'를 의미하며, '이'는 불을 뜻하고, 뜨겁고 밝음을 나타냅니다.

retains both hotness and brightness.

Movements and turns of Poomsae Taegeuk 3 Jang are as follows;

At ready position, Basic Ready Stance looking toward bottom.

[1] Toward top-right, putting forth left foot to step down, Left Side Forward Stance and Low Blocking

[2]-1 Toward top-right, Right Foot Front Kick to step down,

[2]-2/3 Right Side Forward Inflection Stance and Trunk Double Punch

태극 3장의 동작과 순서는 다음과 같습니다.

준비 위치에서 아래 방향을 보며 기본준비서기

[1] 오른쪽 위 방향으로 왼발 내디뎌 왼앞서기 내려막기

[2]–1 오른쪽 위 방향으로 오른발 앞차기 하고 내디뎌

[2]–2/3 오른앞굽이 몸통두번지르기

Words

retain 함유하다, 유지
    하다
hotness 뜨거움
brightness 밝음

[3] Toward top—left, moving back right foot to turn around, Right Side Forward Stance and Low Blocking

[4] Toward top—left, Left Foot Front Kick to step down. Simultaneously, Left Side Forward Inflection Stance and Trunk Double Punch

[5] Toward bottom, moving left foot to step down, Left Side Forward Stance and Hand Blade Neck Hitting

[6] Toward bottom, putting right foot to step down, Right Side Forward Stance and Hand Blade Neck Hitting

[7] Toward middle—right, moving left foot to step down, Right Side Backward Inflection Stance and Single Hand Blade Trunk Outer Blocking

[3] 왼쪽 위 방향으로 오른발 옮겨 뒤로 돌아서 오른앞서기 내려막기

[4] 왼쪽 위 방향으로 왼발 앞차기 하고 내디뎌 왼앞굽이 몸통두번지르기

[5] 아래 방향으로 왼발 옮겨 디뎌 왼앞서기 (목)손날안치기

[6] 아래 방향으로 오른발 내디뎌 오른앞서기 (목)손날안치기

[7] 오른쪽 중간 방향으로 왼발 옮겨 디뎌 오른뒷굽이 (몸통)손날바깥막기

[8] Toward middle−right, putting right foot at their places, push forward left foot half a step to make Left Side Forward Inflection Stance and Trunk Right(Straight) Punch

[9] Toward middle−left, putting left foot at its place to change direction, Left Side Backward Inflection Stance and Single Hand Blade Trunk Outer Blocking

[10] Toward middle−left, putting left foot at its place, push forward right foot half a step to make Right Side Forward Inflection Stance and Trunk Right(Straight) Punch

1.4 Taegeuk 4 Jang

Master   Taegeuk 4 Jang symbolizes the 'Jin' which is one of the 8 divination signs. 'Jin' represents thunder and also holds the meaning of both great power and dignity.

Movements and turns of Poomsae Taegeuk 4 Jang are as follows;

[8] 오른쪽 중간 방향으로 오른발 제자리에 두고 왼발 반발 밀고 나
가 왼앞굽이 몸통바로지르기

[9] 왼쪽 중간 방향으로 왼발 제자리에 두고 방향 바꿔 왼뒷굽이 손
날바깥막기

[10] 왼쪽 중간 방향으로 왼발 제자리에 두고 오른발 반발 밀고 나가
오른앞굽이 몸통바로지르기

1.4 태극 4장

사범   태극 4장은 팔괘의 '진'을 의미하며, '진'은 우레를 나타내고, 또한 큰
힘과 위엄을 내포합니다.

태극 4장의 동작과 순서는 다음과 같습니다.

At ready position, Basic Ready Stance looking toward bottom.

[1] Toward top-right, stepping forth left foot, Right Side Backward Inflection Stance and Hand Blade Blocking.

[2] Toward top-right, put right foot to step down and Press Blocking. Next, Right Side Forward Inflection Stance and Flat Hand Tip Erected(Vertical) Thrusting.

[3] Toward top-left, moving right foot to turn around, Left Side Backward Inflection Stance and Hand Blade Trunk Blocking.

[4] Toward top-left, putting left foot to step down, Left Side Forward Inflection Stance and Flat Hand Tip Erected(Vertical) Thrusting.

준비 위치에서 아래 방향을 보며 기본준비서기

[1] 오른쪽 위 방향으로 왼발 내디뎌 오른뒷굽이 손날거들어바깥막기

[2] 오른쪽 위 방향으로 오른발 내디디며 눌러막기를 하고 오른앞굽이
편손끝세워찌르기

[3] 왼쪽 위 방향으로 오른발 옮겨 뒤로 돌아서 왼뒷굽이 손날거들
어바깥막기

[4] 왼쪽 위 방향으로 왼발 내디디며 눌러막기 하고 왼앞굽이 편손끝
세워찌르기

[5] Toward bottom, moving left foot to turn around, Left Side Forward Inflection Stance and Swallow Shape Hand Knife

[6] Toward bottom, Right Foot Front Kick to step down. Simultaneously, Right Side Forward Inflection Stance and Trunk Erected(Vertical) Punch

[7] Left Foot Side Kick

[8] Right Foot Side Kick to step down and then Left Side Backward Inflection Stance and Hand Blade Blocking.

[9] Toward bottom—left, moving left foot to turn around, Right Side Backward Inflection Stance and Trunk Outer Blocking.

[5] 아래 방향으로 왼발 옮겨 돌아서 왼앞굽이 (목)손날제비품안치기

Words

swallow shape 제비품

[6] 아래 방향으로 오른발 앞차기 하고 내디뎌 오른앞굽이 몸통바로 지르기

[7] 왼발 옆차기

[8] 오른발 옆차기 하고 내디뎌 왼뒷굽이 손날거들어바깥막기

[9] 왼쪽 아래 방향으로 왼발 옮겨 돌아서 오른뒷굽이 몸통바깥막기

[10]−1/2 Toward bottom−left, Right Foot Front Kick to step back to the original position. Continuously, Right Side Backward Inflection Stance and Trunk Inner Blocking.

 1.5 Taegeuk 5 Jang

Master   Taegeuk 5 Jang symbolizes the 'Son' which is one of the 8 divination signs. 'Son' represents wind and means either mighty force or calmness according to its strength and weakness.

For this reason, Taegeuk 5 Jang is the training level for controlling the strength and the weakness of power.

Movements and turns of Poomsae Taegeuk 5 Jang are as follows;

At ready position, Basic Ready Stance looking toward bottom.

[1] Toward top−right, moving left foot to step down, Left Side Forward Inflection Stance and Low Blocking

[10]–1/2 왼쪽 아래 방향으로 오른발 앞차기 하고 제자리로 물러 디뎌
오른뒷굽이 몸통안막기

Words

continuously 이어서
mighty force 위세, 강
한 힘
calmness 고요
strength 강함
weakness 약함
control 조절하다, 다
루다

1.5 태극 5장

사범 태극 5장은 팔괘의 '손'을 의미하며, '손'은 바람을 뜻하고, 바람의 강
약에 따라 위세와 고요의 뜻을 지닙니다.

Expressions

step back 물러나다
for this reason 따라
서, 이런 이유로

따라서 태극 5장은 힘의 강약을 조절하기 위한 수련 단계입니다.

태극 5장의 동작과 순서는 다음과 같습니다.

준비 위치에서 아래 방향을 보며 기본준비서기

[1] 오른쪽 위 방향으로 왼발 옮겨 디뎌 왼앞굽이 내려막기

[2] Toward top-right, drawing in left foot by a step, Left Hand Stance and Hammer Fist Downward Hit

[3] Toward top-left, putting forth right foot to change direction, Right Side Forward Inflection Stance and Low Blocking

[4] Toward top-left, drawing in right foot by a step, Right Hand Stance and Hammer Fist Downward Hit

[5]-1/2 Toward bottom, putting forth left foot to step down, Left Side Forward Inflection Stance and left hand Trunk Inner Blocking. Next, right hand Trunk Inner Blocking

[6]-1 Toward bottom, Right Foot Front Kick and step down,

[2] 오른쪽 위 방향으로 왼발 한걸음 끌어들여 왼서기 메주먹내려
치기

Words

draw 끌어당기다
hammer fist 메주먹
bottom 아래, 바닥

[3] 왼쪽 위 방향으로 오른발 내디뎌 방향 바꿔서 오른앞굽이 내려
막기

[4] 왼쪽 위 방향으로 오른발 한걸음 끌어들여 오른서기 메주먹내려
치기

[5]-1/2 아래 방향으로 왼발 내디뎌 왼앞굽이 왼손 몸통안막기 하고
이어서 오른손 몸통안막기

[6]-1 아래 방향으로 오른발 앞차기 하고 내디뎌

[6]−2/3 Right Side Forward Inflection Stance and Back Fist Front Hit. Next, Trunk Inner Blocking

[7]−1 Toward bottom, Left Foot Front Kick and step down,

[7]−2/3 Left Side Forward Inflection Stance and Back Fist Front Hit. Next, Trunk Inner Blocking

[8] Toward bottom, putting forth right foot to step down, Right Side Forward Inflection Stance and Back Fist Front Hit.

[9] Toward bottom−left, moving left foot to turn around, Right Side Backward Inflection Stance and Single Hand Blade Outer Blocking

[6]–2/3 오른앞굽이 등주먹앞치기 이어서 몸통안막기

Words

back fist 등주먹

[7]–1 아래 방향으로 왼발 앞차기 하고 내디뎌

[7]–2/3 왼앞굽이 등주먹앞치기 이어서 몸통안막기

Expressions

turn around 돌다

[8] 아래 방향으로 오른발 내디뎌 오른앞굽이 등주먹앞치기

[9] 왼쪽 아래 방향으로 왼발 옮겨 돌아서 오른뒷굽이 손날바깥막기

[10] Toward bottom—left, putting forth right foot to step down, Right Side Forward Inflection Stance and Elbow Spiral(Turning) Hit

 1.6 Taegeuk 6 Jang

Master   Taegeuk 6 Jang symbolizes the 'Kam' which is one of the 8 divination signs. 'Kam' represents water and it means continuous flow and softness.

Movements and turns of Poomsae Taegeuk 6 Jang are as follows;

At ready position, Basic Ready Stance looking toward bottom.

[1] Toward top—right, putting forth left foot to step down, Left Side Forward Inflection Stance and Low Blocking

[2] Toward top—right, Right Foot Front Kick to retrieve. Next, Right Side Backward Inflection Stance and Trunk Outer Blocking

[10] 왼쪽 아래 방향으로 오른발 내디뎌 오른앞굽이 팔굽돌려치기

Words

elbow 팔굽(팔꿈치)
continuous 끊임없는
flow 흐름
softness 유연함, 부드
  러움
retrieve 되찾다, 회수
  하다

1.6 태극 6장

사범 태극 6장은 팔괘의 '감'을 의미하며, '감'은 물을 뜻하고, 끊임없는 흐름과 유연함을 뜻합니다.

태극 6장의 동작과 순서는 다음과 같습니다.

준비 위치에서 아래 방향을 보며 기본준비서기

[1] 오른쪽 위 방향으로 왼발을 내디디며 왼앞굽이 내려막기

[2] 오른쪽 위 방향으로 오른발 앞차기 하고 물러 디뎌 오른뒷굽이 몸통바깥막기

[3] Put forth right foot half a step toward top‒left. Next, change direction to make Right Side Forward Inflection Stance and Low Blocking

[4] Toward top‒left, Left Foot Front Kick to retrieve. Next, Left Side Backward Inflection Stance and Trunk Outer Blocking

[5] Toward bottom, moving left foot to step down, Right Side Forward Inflection Stance and Right Single Hand Blade Face Twist Blocking

[6]‒1 Right Foot Face Spiral(Turning) Kick toward bottom direction,

[6]‒2 Put forth the foot one step and a half toward bottom,

[3] 왼쪽 위 방향으로 오른발을 반걸음 내디디며 방향 바꿔 오른앞굽
이 내려막기

Words

twist 비틀다
spiral 나선형의

[4] 왼쪽 위 방향으로 왼발 앞차기 하고 물러 디뎌 왼뒷굽이 몸통바
깥막기

[5] 아래 방향으로 왼발 옮겨 디뎌 왼앞굽이 (얼굴)오른손날비틀어
바깥막기

[6]-1 아래 방향으로 오른발얼굴돌려차기 하고

[6]-2 아래 방향으로 한걸음 반 내디디고

[6]−3 Toward middle−right, moving left foot to step down, Left Side Forward Inflection Stance and Face Outer Blocking. Continuously, Trunk Right(Straight) Punch

[7] Toward middle−right, Right Foot Front Kick to step down, Right Side Forward Inflection Stance and Trunk Right(Straight) Punch

[8] Toward middle−left, moving back right foot to turn around, Right Side Forward Inflection Stance and Face Outer Blocking. Continuously, Trunk Right(Straight) Punch

[9] Toward middle−left, Left Foot Front Kick to step down, Left Side Forward Inflection Stance and Trunk Right(Straight) Punch

[10] Looking toward bottom, putting right foot at its place, pull and move left foot to put it onto middle−right line. Simultaneously, Parallel Stance and Low Scattered Blocking

[6]-3 오른쪽 중간 방향으로 왼발 옮겨 디뎌 왼앞굽이 얼굴바깥막기 이어서 몸통바로지르기

Words

parallel 평행한
scattered blocking 헤
  쳐막기
pull 당기다, 끌다

[7] 오른쪽 중간 방향으로 오른발 앞차기 하고 내디뎌 오른앞굽이 몸통바로지르기

[8] 왼쪽 중간 방향으로 오른발 옮겨 뒤로 돌아서 오른앞굽이 얼굴바깥막기 이어서 몸통바로지르기

[9] 왼쪽 중간 방향으로 왼발 앞차기 하고 내디뎌 왼앞굽이 몸통바로지르기

[10] 아래 방향을 보며 오른발 제자리에 두고 왼발 끌어 옮겨 오른쪽 중간 선상에 딛고 나란히서기 헤쳐내려막기

🎧 ▶ 1.7 1.7 Taegeuk 7 Jang

Master   Taegeuk 7 Jang symbolizes the 'Kan' which is one of the 8 divination signs. 'Kan' represents mountain and means both ponderosity and firmness.

Movements and turns of Poomsae Taegeuk 7 Jang are as follows;

At ready position, Basic Ready Stance looking toward bottom.

[1] Toward top—right, Left Side Tiger Stance and Palm Hand Trunk Inner Blocking

[2]—1/2 Toward top—right, Right Foot Front Kick and retrieve the foot to the original position. Next, Left Side Tiger Stance and Trunk Blocking

[3] Change direction to top—left, Right Side Tiger Stance and Palm Hand Trunk Inner Blocking

1.7 태극 7장

사범 태극 7장은 팔괘의 '간'을 의미하며, '간'은 산을 의미하고, 육중하고
굳건하다는 뜻을 지닙니다.

Words

mountain 산
ponderosity 육중함
firmness 굳건함
tiger 범, 호랑이

태극 7장의 동작과 순서는 다음과 같습니다.

준비 위치에서 아래 방향을 보며 기본준비서기

[1] 오른쪽 위 방향으로 왼범서기 (몸통)오른바탕손안막기

[2]-1/2 오른쪽 위 방향으로 오른발 앞차기 하고 제자리로 물러 디뎌
왼범서기 (몸통)안막기

[3] 왼쪽 위 방향으로 방향 바꿔 오른범서기 (몸통)왼바탕손안막기

[4]−1/2 Toward top−left, Left Foot Front Kick and retrieve the foot to the original position. Next, Right Side Tiger Stance and Trunk Blocking

[5] Toward bottom, putting forth left foot to step down, Right Side Backward Inflection Stance and Hand Blade Low Blocking

[6] Toward bottom, putting forth right foot to step down, Left Side Backward Inflection Stance and Hand Blade Low Blocking

[7] Toward middle−right, move left foot to step down to make Left Side Tiger Stance and Palm Hand Assisted Trunk Inner Blocking

[8]−1/2 Keeping direction onto middle−right, turn upper part of body leftward and then twist rightward. Simultaneously, use impulsive

[4]-1/2 왼쪽 위 방향으로 왼발 앞차기 하고 제자리로 물러 디뎌 오른
범서기 (몸통)안막기

Words

original 원래의
impulsive 충동적인,
자극적인

[5] 아래 방향으로 왼발 내디뎌 오른뒷굽이 손날거들어내려막기

[6] 아래 방향으로 오른발 내디뎌 왼뒷굽이 손날거들어내려막기

[7] 오른쪽 중간 방향으로 왼발 옮겨 디뎌 왼범서기 (몸통)바탕손거들
어안막기

[8]-1/2 오른쪽 중간 방향 그대로 허리를 왼쪽으로 돌렸다 이어서 오
른쪽으로 트는 반작용의 탄력으로 왼범서기 등주먹얼굴앞치기

power of twisting to deliver Left Side Tiger Stance and Back Fist Face Front Hit

[9] Change direction toward middle—left, Right Side Tiger Stance and Palm Hand Assisted Trunk Inner Blocking

[10]—1/2 Keeping direction onto middle—left, turn body rightward and then twist leftward. Simultaneously, use impulsive power of twisting to deliver Right Side Tiger Stance and Back Fist Face Front Hit

 1.8 Taegeuk 8 Jang

Master   Taegeuk 8 Jang symbolizes 'Kon' - one of the 8 divination signs, and means both darkness and earth. 'Kon' also represents root and settlement, as well as both the beginning and the end.

Movements and turns of Poomsae Taegeuk 8 Jang are as follows;

[9] 왼쪽 중간 방향으로 방향을 바꿔 오른범서기 (몸통)바탕손거들어
안막기

[10]–1/2 왼쪽 중간 방향 그대로 몸을 오른쪽으로 돌렸다 이어서 왼쪽
으로 트는 반작용의 탄력으로 오른범서기 등주먹앞치기

1.8 태극 8장

사범 태극 8장은 '곤'을 의미하며, '곤'은 음과 땅을 나타냅니다. '곤'은 또한
뿌리와 안정, 시작과 끝의 의미도 지닙니다.

태극 8장의 동작과 순서는 다음과 같습니다.

At ready position, Basic Ready Stance looking toward bottom.

[1] Toward bottom, putting forth left foot to step down, Right Side Backward Inflection Stance and Assisted Trunk Right(Straight) Blocking

[2] Toward bottom, putting forth left foot half a step, Left Side Forward Inflection Stance and Trunk Right(Straight) Punch

[3]−1 Toward bottom, Left Foot Flying Twin Front Kick,

[3]−2/3 Landing two steps forward to make Left Foot Kick,

준비 위치에서 아래 방향을 보며 기본준비서기

[1] 아래 방향으로 왼발 내디뎌 오른뒷굽이 (몸통)거들어바깥막기

[2] 아래 방향으로 왼발 반발 내디뎌 왼앞굽이 몸통바로지르기

[3]–1 아래 방향으로 오른발부터 두발당성앞차기 하고 (기합)

[3]–2/3 한걸음 앞으로 내려 디뎌, 왼발 차기

Words

basic 기본적인
land 내리다, 착륙하다

[3]–4/5/6 Left Side Forward Inflection Stance and Trunk Blocking. Next, Trunk Double Punch.

[4] Toward bottom, putting forth right foot to step down, Right Side Forward Inflection Stance and Trunk Opposite Punch

[5] Toward bottom–left, moving left foot to turn around, Right Side Forward Inflection Stance and Single Mountain Shape Blocking

[6] Toward bottom–left, putting two feet at their places, move left foot slightly leftward to make Left Side Forward Inflection Stance and Tug and Punch Jaw

[7] Continuously, moving right foot to step down, Left Side Forward Inflection Stance and Single Mountain Shape Blocking

[3]–4/5/6   왼앞굽이 몸통막기 이어서 몸통두번지르기

[4]   아래 방향으로 오른발 내디뎌 오른앞굽이 몸통반대지르기

[5]   왼쪽 아래 방향으로 왼발 옮겨 돌아서 오른앞굽이 외산틀막기

[6]   왼쪽 아래 방향으로 두 다리 제자리에 두고 왼발 왼쪽으로 옮겨
       디뎌 왼앞굽이 (턱)당겨지르기

[7] 오른쪽 아래 방향으로 왼발 옮겨 앞꼬아서기로 딛고 이어서 바로
    오른쪽 아래 방향으로 오른발 옮겨 디뎌 왼앞굽이 외산틀막기

Words

single mountain shape
  blocking 외산틀막기
slightly 약간, 조금
tug 끌어당기다
continuously 이어서,
  연달아

[8] Toward bottom—right, putting two feet at their places, move right foot slightly rightward to make Right Side Forward Inflection Stance and Tug and Punch Jaw

[9] Toward bottom, moving right foot to the ready position direction to step down, Right Side Backward Inflection Stance and Hand Blade Blocking

[10] Toward bottom, pushing forward left foot slightly to step down, Left Side Forward Inflection Stance and Trunk Right(Straight) Punch

[8] 오른쪽 아래 방향으로 두 다리 제자리에 두고 오른발을 오른쪽으로 옮겨 디뎌 오른앞굽이 (턱)당겨지르기

Words

rightward 오른쪽으로
push 밀다

[9] 아래 방향을 향하여 오른발을 준비 위치 방향으로 옮겨 디뎌 오른뒷굽이 손날거들어바깥막기

[10] 아래 방향으로 왼발 반발 밀어서 왼앞굽이 몸통바로지르기

2. Koryo

Master Koryo symbolizes 'Seonbae' which means a learned man.

A learned man is characterized by strong martial spirits and the righteous spirit of learned man.

Movements and turns of Poomsae Koryo are as follows;

At ready position, Pushing Log(Hands) Ready Stance looking toward bottom

[1] Putting forth left foot toward top—right, Hand Blade Blocking and Right Side Backward Inflection Stance

[2]—1 Toward top—right, Low Side Kick with right foot

2. 고려

Words
characterize ~의 특징
  이 되다
martial spirit 무도정신
righteous 올곧은

사범   고려는 지식인이라는 의미의 선배(선비)를 상징하는 말입니다.

지식인은 강한 무도정신과 올곧은 선비의 정신으로 특징지어집니다.

고려의 동작과 순서는 다음과 같습니다.

처음에 준비 위치에서 아래를 바라보며 통밀기 준비서기

[1] 오른쪽 위 방향으로 왼발 내딛고 오른뒷굽이 손날거들어바깥막기

[2]-1 오른쪽 위 방향으로 오른발 한 발로 아래옆차기(무릎)를 하고,

[2]-2 Then, Trunk Side Kick,

[2]-3 Next, take a step and Hand Blade Outer Hit with Right Side Forward Inflection Stance

[3] Toward top-right, withdraw right hand to the waist and Trunk Right Punch with Right Side Forward Inflection Stance

[4] Toward top-right, pull right foot back and Trunk Blocking with Left Side Backward Inflection Stance

[5] Toward top-left, move right foot to turn around and Hand Blade Blocking with Left Side Backward Inflection Stance

[2]-2 이어서 몸통(또는 얼굴)옆차기를 하고,

[2]-3 내디디며 오른앞굽이 손날바깥치기

[3] 오른쪽 위 방향으로 오른손 허리로 잡아당기며 오른앞굽이 몸통
바로지르기

[4] 오른쪽 위 방향으로 오른발 뒤로 끌어 왼뒷굽이 (몸통)안막기

[5] 왼쪽 위 방향으로 오른발 뒤로 돌아 왼뒷굽이 손날거들어바깥
막기

Words

take step (걸음을) 내
딛다
withdraw 잡아당기다,
빼내다

[6]-1 Toward top-left, Low Side Kick with left foot

[6]-2 Then, Trunk Side Kick,

[6]-3 Next, take step and Hand Blade Outer Hit with Left Side Forward Inflection Stance

[7] Toward top-left, withdraw left hand to the waist and Trunk Right Punch with Left Side Forward Inflection Stance

[8] Toward top-left, pull left foot back and Trunk Blocking with Right Side Backward Inflection Stance

[6]-1 왼쪽 위 방향으로 왼발 한 발로 아래(무릎)옆차기를 하고,

Words

low 아래, 낮은
inflection 굽이
pull 당기다
backward 뒤쪽으로

[6]-2 이어서 몸통(또는 얼굴)옆차기를 하고,

[6]-3 내디디며 왼앞굽이 손날바깥치기

[7] 왼쪽 위 방향으로 왼손 허리로 잡아당기며 왼앞굽이 몸통바로지르기

[8] 왼쪽 위 방향으로 왼발 뒤로 끌어 오른뒷굽이 (몸통)안막기

[9]–1 Toward bottom, move left foot to turn around and Left Side Single Hand Blade Low Blocking with Left Side Forward Inflection Stance

[9]–2 Next, Right Side Arc Hand Face Front Hit

[10]–1 Toward bottom, Right Foot Front Kick,

[10]–2 Take step and Right Side Single Hand Blade Low Blocking with Right Side Forward Inflection Stance

[10]–3 Next, Left Side Arc Hand Face Front Hit

[9]-1 아래 방향으로 왼발 옮겨 돌아 왼앞굽이 왼손날내려막기
하고,

[9]-2 이어서 칼재비

[10]-1 아래 방향으로 오른발앞차기 하고,

[10]-2 내디뎌 오른앞굽이 손날내려막기 하고,

[10]-3 이어서 칼재비

Words
arc hand 아금손

Expressions
turn around 돌다

2-(2) [11]-1 Toward bottom, Left Foot Front Kick,

[11]-2 Take step and Left Side Single Hand Blade Low Blocking with Left Side Forward Inflection Stance

[11]-3 Next, Right Side Arc Hand Face Front Hit

[12]-1 Toward bottom, Right Foot Fronk Kick,

[12]-2 Take step and Knee Bending with Right Side Forward Inflection Stance

[11]–1 아래 방향으로 왼발앞차기 하고,

Words

knee bending 무릎꺾기

[11]–2 내디뎌 왼앞굽이 왼손날내려막기 하고,

[11]–3 이어서 칼재비 (기합)

[12]–1 아래 방향으로 오른발앞차기 하고,

[12]–2 내디뎌 오른앞굽이 무릎꺾기

[13] Toward ready position direction, draw left foot slightly forward and turn body to left, Inner Wrist Trunk Scattered Blocking with Right Side Forward Inflection Stance

[14]−1 & 2 Toward top, Left Foot Fronk Kick, and Knee Bending with Left Side Forward Inflection Stance

[15] Toward ready position direction, Inner Wrist Trunk Scattered Blocking with Left Side Forward Stance

[16] Taking left foot as the axis, turn the body rightward and Riding Stance with putting right foot toward the left, and then also Left Side Single Hand Blade Trunk Side Blocking

[17] Two feet at their places, Riding Stance with twisting the upper part of the body leftward, and then Right Fist Target Thrusting

[13] 왼발 아래 방향으로 나와 돌아서 위 방향으로 오른앞굽이 안팔목
헤쳐막기

[14]-1 & 2 위 방향으로 왼발 앞차기하고 왼앞굽이 무릎꺾기

[15] 왼발 아래 방향으로 왼앞서기 안팔목헤쳐막기

[16] 왼발을 축으로 하여 몸을 오른쪽으로 돌려 오른발을 왼쪽 방향
에 디뎌 주춤서기, 왼손날옆막기

[17] 두 발 제자리에 두고 상반신만 왼쪽으로 틀어 주춤서기, 오른주
먹표적지르기

[18]−1 Toward bottom−right, move right foot to make Cross Stance,

[18]−2 At the same time, Left Foot Side Kicking with pulling two fists together

[18]−3 With landing, change direction and Right Side Forward Inflection Stance, and then Left Side Hand Tip Low Bending Backward Thrusting

[19] Left foot at its place, draw in right foot and Low Blocking with Right Side Forward Stance

[20]−1 Toward bottom−left, put forth left foot a step and Left Palm Hand Press Blocking,

[18]-1 오른쪽 아래 방향으로 오른발을 옮겨 앞 꼬아서 옮기기를 하면서,

Words

palm 손바닥
press 누르다

[18]-2 동시에 두 손을 잡아끌며 왼발 옆차기

[18]-3 내려디디며 방향 바꾸어 오른앞굽이, (아래)편손끝당겨젖혀찌르기

Expressions

at the same time 동
    시에
change direction 방향
    을 바꾸다

[19] 왼발 제자리에 두고 오른발 끌어당겨 오른앞서기 내려막기

[20]-1 왼쪽 아래 방향으로 왼발 한걸음 내디디며 왼바탕손눌러막기를 하며,

[20]-2 Put forth right foot again and Right Elbow Side Hit

🎧 2-(3) [21] Toward bottom-left, Riding Stance with two legs at their places, and then Right Single Hand Blade Trunk Side Blocking

[22] Toward bottom-left, Riding Stance with two feet at their places, and then Left Fist Target Punch

[23]-1 Toward bottom-left, move body with its left foot making Forward Cross Stance,

[23]-2 Right Foot Trunk Side Kick with landing,

[20]–2 이어서 오른발을 또 내디뎌 주춤서기 오른팔굽거들어옆치기

Words

elbow 팔굽(팔꿈치)
target punch 표적지
  르기
cross stance 꼬아서기

[21] 왼쪽 아래 방향으로 두 다리 제자리에 두고 주춤서기, (몸통)오른
    손날옆막기

[22] 왼쪽 아래 방향으로 두 발 제자리에 두고 주춤서기, 왼주먹표적
    지르기

[23]–1 왼쪽 아래 방향으로 왼발 옮겨 앞꼬아서기로 몸을 옮기며,

[23]–2 이어서 오른발 옆차기하고 내려딛으며,

[23]-3 Change direction to bottom—right and Left Side Forward Inflection Stance together with Right Side Hand Tip Low Bending Backward Thrusting

[24] Right foot at its place, pull left foot toward bottom—right and Left Side Forward Stance Low Blocking

[25]-1 Put forth right foot a step toward bottom—right and Right Palm Hand Press Blocking.

[25]-2 Put forth left foot a step and Riding Stance Left Elbow Side Hit

[26] Looking toward bottom, put left foot at its place. Draw right foot and Cross Stance. Left Hammer Fist Low Target Hit

[23]–3 오른쪽 아래 방향으로 바꿔 왼앞굽이 (아래)오른편손끝당겨찌
르기

Words

thrust 찌르기
palm hand 바탕손
cross stance 꼬아서기
hammer fist 메주먹

[24] 오른발 제자리에 두고 오른쪽 아래 방향으로 왼발 끌어 왼앞서
기 내려막기

[25]–1 오른쪽 아래 방향으로 오른발 한걸음 내디뎌 오른바탕손눌러
막기 하고,

[25]–2 이어서 왼발을 한걸음 내디뎌 주춤서기 왼팔굽옆치기

[26] 아래 방향을 바라보며 왼발 제자리. 모둠발로 오른발 끌어들여
모아서기. 왼메주먹아래표적치기

[27]–1 At bottom position, turn body to left and Left Single Hand Blade Outer Hit

[27]–2 Looking toward ready position, put forth left foot. Left Side Forward Cross Stance and Left Single Hand Blade Low Blocking

[28]–1 Putting forth right foot toward ready position, Right Side Forward Inflection Stance and Right Single Hand Blade Neck Hit(Hand Knife).

[28]–2 Next, Right Single Hand Blade Low Blocking

[29]–1 Putting forth left foot toward ready position, Left Side Forward Inflection Stance and Left Single Hand Blade Neck Hit.

[27]-1 아래 위치에서 몸을 왼쪽으로 돌려 왼앞굽이 (왼)엎은손날바깥치기

[27]-2 이어서 왼손날내려막기

Words

hand blade(hand knife)
  손날
inflection 굽이
cross stance 꼬아서기

[28]-1 준비 위치 방향으로 오른발 내디뎌 오른앞굽이 (목)오른손날목치기 하고,

[28]-2 이어서 오른손날내려막기

[29]-1 준비위치 방향으로 왼발 내디뎌 왼앞굽이 (목)왼손날안치기 하고,

[29]-2 Next, Left Single Hand Blade Low Blocking

[30]-1 Putting forth right foot toward ready position, Right Side Forward Inflection Stance and Right Side Arc Hand Face Front Hit.

[30]-2 At ready position, put right foot at its place. Turn body to left and draw left foot. Look toward bottom and Pushing Log(Hands) Ready Stance

3. Keumgang

Master Keumkang has the meaning of hardness and ponderosity.

Both the Mt. Keumkang and Keumkang-Yeoksa are the background of Keumkang Poomsae. Mt. Keumkang has been regarded as the center of national martial spirit and Keumkang Yeoksa

[29]-2 이어서 왼손날내려막기

Words

arc hand 아금손
pushing log 통밀기
hardness 강함
ponderosity 무거움
background 배경
martial spirit 무도정신

[30]-1 준비위치 방향으로 오른발 내디뎌 오른앞굽이 오른칼재비
하고 (기합)

[30]-2 준비위치에서 오른발 제자리, 몸을 왼쪽으로 돌려 왼발을 끌
어 아래 방향을 바라보며 통밀기준비서기

Expressions

regard as ~로 여기다

3. 금강

사범   금강이란 강함과 무거움을 나타냅니다.

금강을 이루는 배경은 우리나라 무도정신의 중심으로 여겨지는 금강
산과 용맹한 전사를 의미하는 금강역사로 이뤄져 있습니다.

represents a mightiest warrior.

Movements and turns of Poomsae Keumkang are as follows;

At ready position, Basic Ready Stance looking toward bottom direction.

[1] Putting forth left foot toward bottom, Left Side Forward Inflection Stance and Inner Wrist Trunk Scattered Blocking

[2] Putting forth right foot toward bottom, Right Side Forward Inflection Stance and Right Palm Hand Jaw Hitting

[3] Putting forth left foot toward bottom, Left Side Forward Inflection Stance and Left Palm Hand Jaw Hitting

금강의 동작과 순서는 다음과 같습니다.

준비 위치에서 아래 방향을 보며 기본준비서기

[1] 아래 방향으로 왼발 내디뎌 왼앞굽이 안팔목헤쳐막기

[2] 아래 방향으로 오른발 내디뎌 오른앞굽이 (턱)오른바탕손앞치기

[3] 아래 방향으로 왼발 내디뎌 왼앞굽이 (턱)왼바탕손앞치기

Words

represent ~를 의미
  하다
mightiest warrior 용
  맹한 전사
scattered blocking 헤
  쳐막기

[4] Putting forth right foot toward bottom, Right Side Forward Inflection Stance and Right Palm Hand Jaw Hitting

[5] Retrieving backward right foot toward bottom to step down, Right Side Backward Inflection Stance and Single Hand Blade Trunk Blocking

[6] Retrieving backward left foot toward bottom to step down, Left Side Backward Inflection Stance and Single Hand Blade Trunk Blocking

[7] Retrieving backward right foot toward bottom to step down, Right Side Backward Inflection Stance and Single Hand Blade Trunk Blocking

[8] Putting right foot at ready position, toward top−right, Right Side Crane Stance and Diamond Blocking

[4] 아래 방향으로 오른발 내디뎌 오른앞굽이 (턱)오른바탕손앞치기

[5] 위 방향으로 오른발 뒤로 물러 디뎌 오른뒷굽이 왼손날안막기

[6] 위 방향으로 왼발 뒤로 물러 디뎌 왼뒷굽이 오른손날안막기

[7] 위 방향으로 오른발 뒤로 물러 디뎌 오른뒷굽이 왼손날안막기

[8] 오른발은 준비 위치에 그대로 두고 오른쪽 위 방향으로 오른학다
리서기 금강막기

Words

retrieve 되찾다, 회수
하다
crane stance 학다리
서기
diamond blocking 금
강막기

[9] Put forth left foot to step down toward top—right, Riding Stance and Large Hinge

[10] Turn body to left toward top—right direction and move right foot to step down onto top—right line. Next, moving left foot also onto top—right line, Riding Stance and Large Hinge

4. Taebaek

Master   Taebaek is the name of a bright mountain where Dan-gun founded the nation of Korean people.

A bright mountain symbolizes sacredness of soul and Dan-gun's thought of humanitarian ideal.

Movements and turns of Poomsae Taebaek are as follows;

At ready position, looking toward bottom direction, Basic Ready Stance

[9] 오른쪽 위 방향으로 왼발 내려디뎌 주춤서기 큰돌쩌귀

Words

large hinge 큰돌쩌귀
found (나라를) 세우다
sacredness 신성함
humanitarian 홍익인
　간의, 인도주의적인

[10] 오른쪽 위 방향으로 몸을 왼쪽으로 돌려서 오른발로 오른쪽 위
　　선상에 옮겨 딛고, 이어서 왼발을 또 오른쪽 위 선상에 옮겨 디뎌
　　주춤서기 큰돌쩌귀

4. 태백

사범　태백은 한민족의 고대국가를 개국한 단군왕검이 있던 밝은산을 의미
　　합니다.

　　밝은산은 얼의 신성함과 단군의 홍익인간 사상을 상징합니다.

　　태백의 동작과 순서는 다음과 같습니다.

　　준비 위치에서 아래 방향을 바라보며 기본준비서기

[1] Turning body toward top–right, Left Side Tiger Stance and Hand Blade Low Scattered Blocking

[2] Toward top–right, Right Foot Front Kick to step down. Next, Right Side Forward Inflection Stance and Trunk Double Punch (quickly)

[3] Toward top–left, move right foot to turn around. Next, Right Side Tiger Stance and Hand Blade Low Scattered Blocking

[4] Toward top–left, Left Foot Front Kick to step down. Next, Left Side Forward Inflection Stance and Trunk Double Punch (quickly)

[5] Toward bottom, move left foot to turn. Next, Left Side Forward Inflection Stance and Swallow Shape Hand Knife

[1] 오른쪽 위 방향으로 왼범서기 (아래)손날헤쳐막기

Words

tiger stance 범서기
scattered blocking 헤
 쳐막기
swallow shape 제비품

[2] 오른쪽 위 방향으로 오른발 앞차기 하고 내디뎌 오른앞굽이 몸통
두번지르기 (빠르게)

[3] 왼쪽 위 방향으로 오른발 옮겨 뒤로 돌아 오른범서기 (아래)손날
헤쳐막기

[4] 왼쪽 위 방향으로 왼발앞차기 하고 내디뎌 왼앞굽이 몸통두번지
르기 (빠르게)

[5] 아래 방향으로 왼발 옮겨 돌아 왼앞굽이 (목)제비품안치기

[6]−1 Toward bottom, twist right hand wrist outward from inside and, simultaneously, and pull the opponent's wrist,

[6]−2 Next, putting forth right foot to step down, Right Side Forward Inflection Stance and Trunk Right(Straight) Punch

[7]−1 Toward bottom, twist left hand wrist inside,

[7]−2 Next, putting forth left foot to step down, Left Side Forward Inflection Stance and Trunk Right(Straight) Punch

[8]−1 Toward bottom, twist right hand wrist outward from inside and, simultaneously, grab and pull the opponent,

[6]-1 아래 방향으로 오른손목을 안으로 젖혀 틀면서 상대의 손목을
잡아끌며,

Words

simultaneously 동시에
grab 잡다
inflection 굽이
twist 비틀다

[6]-2 오른발 내디뎌 오른앞굽이 몸통바로지르기

[7]-1 아래 방향으로 왼손목을 안으로 젖혀내며,

[7]-2 왼발 내디뎌 왼앞굽이 몸통바로지르기

[8]-1 아래 방향으로 오른손목을 안으로 젖혀내며 상대를 잡아끌며,

[8]−2 Putting forth right foot to step down, and Right Side Forward Inflection Stance and Trunk Right(Straight) Punch

[9] Toward bottom−left, move left foot to turn. Next, Right Side Backward Inflection Stance and Diamond Trunk Blocking

[10] Toward bottom−left, put two feet at their place. Next, Right Side Backward Inflection Stance and Tug and Punch Jaw

5. Pyongwon

Master Pyongwon means the plain and vast stretched-out land.

Pyongwon is the source of life for all the creatures and the field where human beings live their lives.

Movements and turns of Poomsae Pyongwon are as follows;

[8]–2 오른발 내디뎌 오른앞굽이 몸통바로지르기 (기합)

[9] 왼쪽 아래 방향으로 왼발 옮겨 돌아 오른뒷굽이 (몸통)안팔목금강
  바깥막기

[10] 왼쪽 아래 방향으로 두 발 제자리에 두고, 오른뒷굽이 (턱)당겨
  지르기

5. 평원

사범   평원은 넓게 펼쳐진 큰 땅을 의미합니다.

평원은 모든 생명의 삶을 위한 근원이 되며, 동시에 인간의 삶의 터전
인 곳입니다.

평원의 동작과 순서는 다음과 같습니다.

At ready position, looking toward bottom, Close Stance and Overlapped Hands Ready Stance

[1] Toward bottom, open left foot a step wide. Next, Parallel Stance and Hand Blade Low Scattered Blocking

[2] Toward bottom, two feet at their places, gather two hands in front of the chest. Simultaneously, keeping the palm face to face with each other, Parallel Stance and Pushing Log(Hands)

[3] Toward left, put forth right foot to step down. Next, Left Side Backward Inflection Stance and Single Hand Blade Low Blocking

[4] Change direction toward right, Right Side Backward Inflection Stance and Single Hand Blade Trunk Outer Blocking

준비 위치에서 아래 방향을 보며 모아서기 겹손준비서기

[1] 아래 방향으로 왼발 한 발 너비로 넓혀 나란히서기 (아래)손날헤쳐막기

[2] 아래 방향으로 두 발 제자리에 두고 두 손을 단전 앞에서 가슴 앞으로 들어 올리면서 손바닥을 마주보게 하며 나란히 서기 통밀기 (인중높이)

[3] 왼쪽 방향으로 오른발 내디뎌 왼뒷굽이 오른손날내려막기

[4] 오른쪽 방향으로 방향 바꾸며 오른뒷굽이 왼손날바깥막기

Words

overlap 겹치다
gather 모으다
chest 가슴

Expressions

in front of~ ~의 앞에
face to face 마주보고

[5] Toward right, push left foot slightly forward. Simultaneously, Left Side Backward Inflection Stance and Right Elbow Lifting Hit

[6]-1 Toward right, Right Foot Front Kick and step down.

[6]-2 Successively, (with right foot being the axis) Left Foot Trunk Spiral(Turning) Side Kick.

[6]-3 Stepping down at right position, Left Side Backward Inflection Stance and Hand Blade Blocking

[7] Toward left, putting two feet at their places, Left Side Backward Inflection Stance and Hand Blade Low Blocking

[5] 오른쪽 방향으로 왼발 밀고 나가며 왼앞굽이 오른팔굽올려치기

Words

elbow 팔굽(팔꿈치)
successively 이어서
axis 축

[6]-1 오른쪽 방향으로 오른발 앞차기 하고 내려 디뎌

[6]-2 이어서 (오른발을 축으로 하여) 왼발 몸 돌며 옆차기하고,

[6]-3 오른쪽 위치에 내려디뎌 왼뒷굽이 손날거들어바깥막기

[7] 왼쪽 방향으로 두발 제자리에 두고 왼뒷굽이 손날거들어내려막기

[8] Toward left, putting two feet at their places, Riding Stance

[9]−1 Riding Stance and Right Back Fist Tug and Hit Jaw

[9]−2 Simultaneously, Left Back Fist Tug and Hit Jaw

[10] Toward left, putting right foot at its place, move left foot. Simultaneously, Forward Cross Stance and Yoke Hit(Hitting)

[8] 왼쪽 방향으로 오른발 옮겨 주춤서며 (얼굴)거들어옆막기

Words

tug 당기다
cross stance 꼬아서기
yoke hit 멍에치기

[9]-1 주춤서기 (턱)오른등주먹앞치기 (기합)

[9]-2 이어서 (턱)왼등주먹앞치기

[10] 왼쪽 방향으로 오른발 제자리에 두고 왼발을 옮겨 앞꼬아서기 멍
    에치기

6. Sipjin

Master   Sipjin was derived from the thought of longevity and means ten creatures of long life - namely, sun, moon, mountain, water, stone, pine tree, herb of eternal youth, tortoise, deer, and crane.

Sipjin also gives human beings faith, hope, and love. For this reason, they symbolize and change such values.

Movements and turns of Poomsae Sipjin are as follows;

At the center of ready position, looking toward bottom, Basic Ready Stance

[1] Looking toward bottom, put two feet at their places. Simultaneously, raising up two fists, Parallel Stance and Bull Blocking

[2] Toward right direction, open two fists sideward to hold for an instance. Next, looking toward bottom, put forth left foot onto right direction

6. 십진

사범 십진은 십장사상에서 유래된 십장생을 의미하며, 해, 달, 산, 물, 돌, 소나무, 불로초, 거북, 사슴, 학을 일컫습니다.

또한 십진은 사람들에게 믿음, 희망, 사랑을 심어주며, 이러한 것들을 상징하고 변화하는 품새입니다.

십진의 동작과 순서는 다음과 같습니다.

가운데 준비 위치에서 아래 방향을 보며 기본준비서기

[1] 아래 방향을 바라보며 두 발 그대로 두고 두 주먹 올려 나란히서기 황소막기

[2] 두 주먹 양 옆으로 벌려 약간 멈추고, 왼발을 오른쪽 선상에 내디뎌 오른뒷굽이 (몸통)안팔목손바닥거들어바깥막기

Words

longevity 장수
pine tree 소나무
tortoise 거북
deer 사슴
crane 학
bull blocking 황소막기

Expressions

derived from ～에서 유래하다

line. Simultaneously, Right Side Backward Inflection Stance and Palm—assisted Trunk Outer Blocking

[3]—1/2/3 Right Side Hand Tip Downward Thrusting followed by Trunk Double Punch

[4] Toward right, turning body to the left, put forth right foot to step down and Scattered Mountain Shape Blocking

[5] Toward right, move left foot to make Forward Cross(Twist) Stance. Next, moving right foot to step down, Riding Stance and Side Punch

[6] Toward left, turn body to the left and put left foot at its place. Next, moving right foot to step down, Riding Stance and Yoke Hitting

Words

mountain shape blocking 산틀막기
yoke hitting 멍에치기

[3]-1/2/3 오른편손끝엎어찌르기 이어서 몸통두번지르기

[4] 오른쪽 방향으로 몸을 왼쪽으로 돌려 오른발 내디뎌 주춤서기로 헤쳐산틀막기

[5] 오른쪽 방향으로 왼발 옮겨 앞꼬아서기 하고 이어서 오른발을 옮겨 디뎌 주춤서기 옆지르기 (기합)

[6] 왼쪽 방향으로 몸을 왼쪽으로 돌아 왼발 제자리에 두고, 오른발 옮겨 디뎌 주춤서기 멍에치기

[7] At the same time, putting forth right foot onto left direction line to step down, Left Side Backward Inflection Stance and Palm-assisted Trunk Outer Blocking

[8]-1 Toward left, push forward right foot slightly to make Right Side Forward Inflection Stance, Left Side Hand Tip Downward Punch

[8]-2/3 Next, Trunk Double Punch

[9] Toward left, putting forth left foot to step down, Riding Stance and Scattered Mountain Shape Blocking

[10] Toward left, make Right Foot Forward Cross (Twist) Stance. Next, moving left foot to step down onto left direction line, Riding Stance and Trunk Side Punch

[7] 이어서 오른발을 왼쪽 방향 선상에 내디뎌 왼뒷굽이 안팔목손바 닥거들어바깥막기

Words
palm-assisted blocking
손바닥거들어막기

[8]-1 왼쪽 방향으로 안으로 틀어 오른발 밀고 나가 오른앞굽이, 왼편 손끝엎어찌르기

Expressions
at the same time 동
시에

[8]-2/3 이어서, 몸통두번찌르기

[9] 왼쪽 방향으로 왼발 내디뎌 주춤서기 헤쳐산틀막기

[10] 왼쪽 방향으로 오른발앞꼬아서기 하고, 이어서 왼발을 왼쪽방향 선상에 옮겨 디뎌 주춤서기 몸통옆지르기 (기합)

7. Jitae

Master Jitae means a man who is looking over the sky and standing on the ground with two feet.

A man on the earth represents the way of struggling for life such as kicking, treading, and jumping on the ground. Thus, Jitae symbolizes various aspects of human being's struggle for existence.

Movements and turns of Poomsae Jitae are as follows;

At ready position, looking toward bottom, Basic Ready Stance

[1] Toward right, putting forth left foot to step down, Right Side Backward Inflection Stance and Inner Wrist Trunk Outer Blocking

[2] Toward right, putting forth right foot to step down, Right Side Forward Inflection Stance

7. 지태

Words

tread 디디다, 밟다
aspect 양상, 측면
existence 존재, 실재

사범   지태는 사람이 하늘을 향해 두 발을 딛고 선 지상인을 의미합니다.

지상인은 두 발로 차고 밟고 뛰는 삶과 싸움을 나타내고, 생존경쟁 속에서 나타나는 여러 양상을 동작으로 만든 것이 지태입니다.

지태의 동작과 순서는 다음과 같습니다.

Expressions

struggle for~ ~을 위해 싸우다

준비 위치에서 아래 방향을 보며 기본준비서기

[1] 오른쪽 방향으로 왼발 내디뎌 오른뒷굽이 안팔목바깥막기

[2] 오른쪽 방향으로 오른발 내디뎌 오른앞굽이 얼굴막기, 이어서 몸통바로지르기

and Face Blocking. Next, Trunk Right(Straight) Blocking

[3] Toward left, move right foot to step down and turn around. Simultaneously, Left Side Backward Inflection Stance and Inner Wrist Trunk Outer Blocking

[4] Toward left, putting left foot to step down, Left Side Forward Inflection Stance and Face Blocking. Next, Trunk Right(Straight) Punch

[5] Toward ready position direction, moving left foot to turn around, Left Side Forward Inflection Stance and Low Blocking.

[6] Toward top, retrieving back left foot slightly to step down, Right Side Backward Inflection Stance and Left Single Hand Blade Face Blocking

[3] 왼쪽 방향으로 오른발 옮겨 디뎌 뒤로 돌아서 왼뒷굽이 안팔목바
깥막기

Words

simultaneously 동시에
retrieve 끌어당기다,
회수하다

[4] 왼쪽 방향으로 왼발 내디뎌 왼앞굽이 얼굴막기 하고, 이어서 몸통
바로지르기

Expressions

turn around 돌다

[5] 준비 위치 방향으로 왼발 옮겨서 돌아 왼앞굽이 내려막기

[6] 위 방향으로 왼발 약간 끌어당겨, 오른뒷굽이 왼손날올려막기

[7] Toward bottom, Right Foot Front Kick to step down, next, Left Side Backward Inflection Stance and Hand Blade Low Blocking

[8] Toward bottom, putting two feet at their places, Left Side Backward Inflection Stance and Trunk Outer Blocking

[9] Toward bottom, Left Foot Front Kick to step down, next, Right Side Backward Inflection Stance and Hand Blade Low Blocking

[10] Toward bottom, pushing forward left foot slightly, Left Side Forward Inflection Stance and Face Blocking.

[7] 아래 방향으로 오른발 앞차기하고 내디뎌 왼뒷굽이 손날거들어내려막기

Words
push 밀다
slightly 약간

[8] 아래 방향으로 두 다리 제자리에 두고 왼뒷굽이 (몸통)바깥막기

[9] 아래 방향으로 왼발 앞차기하고 내디뎌 오른뒷굽이 손날거들어내려막기

[10] 아래 방향으로 왼발 밀고 나가서 왼앞굽이 얼굴막기

8. Chonkwon

Master   Chonkwon is the origin of all the creatures and also the cosmos itself.

It means the Heaven's Great Mighty, so its infinite competence signifies the creation, change and completion.

Movements and turns of Poomsae Chonkwon are as follows;

At ready position, looking toward bottom, Close Stance and Overlapped Hands Ready Stance

[1] At ready position, putting two feet at their places, Close Stance and Wing Spreading

[2] Toward bottom, retrieving back left foot to step down, Right Side Tiger Stance and Knuckle Protruding Punch

8. 천권

사범   천권은 만물의 근본이자 우주이기도 하며, 하늘이 가진 대능력을 의미합니다.

그 무한한 능력은 창조, 변화와 완성을 나타냅니다.

천권의 동작과 순서는 다음과 같습니다.

준비 위치에서 아래 방향을 보며 모아서기 겹손준비서기

[1] 준비 위치에서 두 다리 제자리에 두고 모아서기 날개펴기

[2] 위 방향으로 왼발 뒤로 물러디뎌 오른범서기 두밤주먹치지르기

Words

origin 근원
cosmos 우주
great mighty 대능력
infinite 무한한
competence 능력, 역량
signify 의미하다, 뜻
   하다
completion 완성
knuckle protruding
   punch 밤주먹

[3] Toward bottom, stepping forward right foot, Right Side Forward Inflection Stance and Single Hand Blade Twist Blocking

[4] Toward bottom, putting forth left foot to step down, catch and pull left hand to make Left Side Forward Inflection Stance and Trunk Right(Straight) Punch

[5] Toward bottom, putting two feet at their places, Left Side Forward Inflection Stance and Single Hand Blade Twist Blocking

[6] Toward bottom, putting forth right foot to step down, catch and pull right hand to make Right Side Forward Inflection Stance and Trunk Right(Straight) Punch

[7] Putting two feet at their places, Right Side Forward Inflection Stance and Single Hand Blade Twist Blocking

[3] 아래 방향으로 오른발을 앞으로 내디뎌 오른앞굽이 손날비틀어바
깥막기

[4] 아래 방향으로 왼발 내디디며 왼손 감아 잡아끌면서 왼앞굽이 몸
통바로지르기

[5] 아래 방향으로 두 다리 제자리에 두고 왼앞굽이 손날비틀어바
깥막기

[6] 아래 방향으로 오른발 내디디며 오른손 감아 잡아끌면서 오른앞
굽이 몸통바로지르기

[7] 두 다리 제자리에 두고 오른앞굽이 손날비틀어바깥막기

[8] Toward bottom, Left Foot Side Kick to step down to make Left Side Forward Inflection Stance and Low Blocking

[9] Toward bottom, putting forth right foot to step down, Right Side Forward Inflection Stance and Trunk Opposite Punch

[10] Toward bottom–left, moving left foot to turn around, Right Side Backward Inflection Stance and Inner Wrist Assisted Trunk Outer Blocking

9. Hansu

Master Hansu means water which is the source of substance preserving the life of all the creatures and growing them.

This water 'Hansu' symbolizes birth and growth of a life, strength and weakness, magnanimity, harmony, and adaptability.

[8] 아래 방향으로 왼발 옆차기(기합)하고 내디뎌 왼앞굽이 내려막기

[9] 아래 방향으로 오른발 내디디며 오른앞굽이 몸통반대지르기

[10] 왼쪽 아래 방향으로 왼발 옮겨 돌아 오른뒷굽이 안팔목거들어바 깥막기

Words

opposite 반대의
substance 물질
preserve 보존하다
grow 자라다
birth 탄생
growth 성장
strength 강함
weakness 약함
magnanimity 포용
harmony 융화
adaptability 적응

9. 한수

사범 한수는 만물의 생명을 유지하고 키워주는 근원이 되는 물질로서 물을 의미합니다.

이는 생명의 탄생과 성장, 강함과 약함, 포용력과 융화력 그리고 적응력을 나타냅니다.

Movements and turns of Poomsae Hansu are as follows;

At the center of ready position, looking toward bottom, Close Stance and Overlapped Hands Ready Stance

[1] Toward bottom, putting forth left foot to step down, Left Side Forward Inflection Stance and Hand Blade Back Trunk Scattered Blocking

[2] Toward bottom, putting forth right foot to step down, Right Side Forward Inflection Stance and Two Hammer Fist Side Hitting

[3] Looking toward bottom, retrieve right foot to ready position to make Right Side Forward Inflection Stance and Single Mountain Shape Blocking

한수의 동작과 순서는 다음과 같습니다.

가운데 준비 위치에서 아래 방향을 보며 모아서기 겹손준비서기

Words

center 중앙
scattered blocking 헤
 쳐막기
hammer fist 메주먹
retrieve 되찾아오다
single mountain shape
 blocking 외산틀막기

[1] 아래 방향으로 왼발 내디뎌 왼앞굽이 (몸통)손날등헤쳐막기

[2] 아래 방향으로 오른발 내디디며 오른앞굽이 두메주먹안치기

[3] 아래 방향을 바라보며 오른발을 가운데 준비 위치에 물러나 디디
 며 오른앞굽이 외산틀막기

[4] Toward bottom, putting two feet at their places, Left Side Forward Inflection Stance and Right(Straight) Punch

[5] Looking toward bottom, retrieve back left foot onto top direction line to make Left Side Forward Inflection Stance and Single Mountain Shape Blocking

[6] Toward bottom, putting two feet at their places, Right Side Forward Inflection Stance and Trunk Right(Straight) Punch

[7] Looking toward bottom, retrieve back right foot onto top direction line to make Right Side Forward Inflection Stance and Single Mountain Shape Blocking

[8] Toward bottom, putting two feet at their places, Left Side Forward Inflection Stance and Trunk Right(Straight) Punch

[4] 아래 방향으로 두 다리 제자리에 두고 왼앞굽이 바로지르기

Words

direction 방향

[5] 아래 방향을 바라보며 왼발을 위쪽 방향 선상으로 뒤로 물러 디
며 왼앞굽이 외산틀막기

[6] 아래 방향으로 두 발 제자리에 두고 오른앞굽이 몸통바로지르기

[7] 아래 방향을 바라보며 오른발을 위쪽 방향선상으로 뒤로 물러 디
며 오른앞굽이 외산틀막기

[8] 아래 방향으로 두 발 제자리에 두고 왼앞굽이 몸통바로지르기

[9] Toward bottom, putting forth right foot to step down, Right Side Forward Inflection Stance and Hand Blade Back Trunk Scattered Blocking

[10] Right foot at ready position, put forth left foot to make Left Side Forward Inflection Stance. Simultaneously, toward diagonal-right, right hand assiting Left Arc Hand Face Front Hit

10. Ilyo

Master Ilyeo means the philosophy of a great Buddhist priest at Silla Dynasty, Saint Wonhyo. The essential thought of his philosophy is characterized by the oneness of both mind (spirit) and body (material).

Movements and turns of Poomsae Ilyeo are as follows;

At ready position, Close Stance and Covered Fist Ready Stance with looking toward bottom direction

[9] 아래 방향으로 오른발 앞으로 내디뎌 오른앞굽이 (몸통)손날등헤 쳐막기

[10] 오른발을 준비 위치에 두고 왼발을 내디뎌 왼앞굽이하고 오른쪽 대각선쪽으로 오른손 눌러막고 거들어 칼재비

10. 일여

사범 일여는 신라의 위대한 승려 원효대사의 사상을 의미하며, 원효사상의 정수는 마음과 몸이 하나라는 것입니다.

일여의 동작과 순서는 다음과 같습니다.

준비 위치에서 아래 방향을 바라보며 모아서기 보주먹 준비서기

[1] Putting forth left foot toward bottom, Right Side Backward Inflection Stance and Hand Blade Blocking

[2] Putting forth right foot toward bottom, Right Side Forward Inflection Stance and Trunk Opposite Punch

[3] Moving left foot to step down toward bottom−right, Right Side Backward Inflection Stance and Diamond Blocking

[4] Moving left foot to turn toward ready position, Right Side Backward Inflection Stance and Hand Blade Blocking

[5] Putting two feet at their place toward ready position, Right Side Backward Inflection Stance and Trunk Straight Punch

[1] 아래 방향으로 왼발 내디뎌 오른뒷굽이 손날거들어바깥막기

Words

opposite 반대의
backward 뒤쪽으로
diamond blocking 금
  강막기

[2] 아래 방향으로 오른발 내디뎌 오른앞굽이 몸통반대지르기

[3] 오른쪽 아래 방향으로 왼발 옮겨디뎌 오른뒷굽이 금강막기

[4] 준비 위치 방향으로 왼발 옮겨 돌아서 오른뒷굽이 손날거들어바
  깥막기

[5] 준비 위치 방향으로 두 발 제자리에 두고 오른뒷굽이 몸통바로
  지르기

[6] Jumping right foot to step down toward ready position, Right Foot Reverse Cross Stance and Assisted Left Side Hand Tip Trunk Erected (Vertical) Thrusting

[7] Putting right foot at its place, slowly Left Foot Side Kick toward top direction. Simultaneously, Right-legged Single Stance and Single Mountain Shape Blocking

[8] Stepping down left foot onto top line, Right Side Backward Inflection Stance and Crossing Face Blocking

[9] Toward top direction, twist and draw the opponent's trapped wrists. Simultaneously, put forth right foot and Right Side Forward Inflection Stance together with Trunk Opposite Punch

[10] Move left foot to step down toward middle-left direction. Simultaneously, Right Side Backward Inflection Stance and Diamond Blocking

[6] 준비 위치 방향으로 오른발 뛰어나가 디디며 오른발오금서기 거들어 왼편손끝거들어세워찌르기 (기합)

Words

erect 세우다
vertical 수직의
simultaneously 동시에
opponent 상대, 적
wrist 팔목

[7] 오른발 제자리에 두고 위 방향으로 서서히 왼발옆차기 하면서 동시에 오른발외다리서며 외산틀막기

[8] 옆차기한 왼발을 위 선상에 내려디디며 오른뒷굽이 엇걸어올려막기

[9] 위 방향으로 엇갈린 상대의 팔목을 비틀어 잡아끌며 오른발 내디며 오른앞굽이 몸통반대지르기

[10] 왼쪽 중간 방향으로 왼발 옮겨디뎌 오른뒷굽이 금강막기

Part 4
Kyorugi

겨루기

Master   Hello everyone, it's been a long time!

Disciple   Yes, master. How have you been?

Master   I've been okay. Meanwhile, today is a meaningful day because we finally get to learn the last part 'Kyorugi' through all the various exercises of basic movements and Poomsae.

Disciple   You bet. We are happy indeed. We should celebrate together this afternoon after the final class!

Master   That's a good idea. Shall we ask our class president to reserve a proper place for the party?

Class President   Yes, master. I will.

Master   Good, let's start our final class then. Kyorugi stands for the whole of Taekwondo techniques.

Kyorugi, based on Taekwondo spirit and founded with basic movements and Poomsae, trains the techniques of both attack(offense) and defense so finally aims to strive for superiority against the opponent.

There are many types of Kyorugi and they are as follows;

사범   여러분, 오랜만입니다!

문하생   네, 사범님. 어떻게 지내셨습니까?

사범   저는 잘 지냈어요. 그런데 오늘은 정말 뜻 깊은 날인데요, 그동안 여러 기본동작들과 품새를 배워왔고, 마침내 마지막 부분인 겨루기를 배우게 되었습니다.

문하생   네, 정말 기쁩니다. 마지막 수업 마치고 오후에 같이 축하해야겠네요!

사범   좋은 생각입니다. 반장이 회식을 위한 마땅한 장소를 찾아봐 주시겠습니까?

반장   네, 사범님. 그렇게 하겠습니다.

사범   좋아요, 그럼 마지막 수업을 시작하도록 하죠. 겨루기는 태권도 기술의 종합적인 집합체라고 보시면 됩니다.

겨루기는 태권도 정신에 입각하여 기본동작과 품새에 토대를 두고 공격과 방어 기술을 수련하며, 궁극적으로 상대방에 대한 우위를 가리기 위해 노력하는 것입니다.

겨루기에는 열두 가지 유형이 있으며, 다음과 같습니다.

Words

meanwhile 그런데
meaningful 의미있는
various 다양한
celebrate 축하하다
class president 반장
reserve 예약하다
proper 적당한

Expressions

stand for~ ~를 대표하다
aim to~ ~를 목표로하다

1. Three-step Kyorugi (Trunk)

Master   This is the basic of Kyorugi and both partners train together according to their arranged manner and order. First, one person attacks the opponent's trunk three times as the other defends by using either hand blade or wrist. After the movement, the other person counter attacks accordingly.

2. Three-step Kyorugi (Face)

Master   At the three-step Kyorugi, both partners aim to attack their opponents' face.

1. 세 번 겨루기(몸통)

사범   겨루기의 기초로서 상대방과 정해진 규칙에 따라 사전에 약속한 대로 수련하는 것을 말합니다. 즉, 내가 먼저 상대방의 몸통을 세 번 공격하면 방어자는 손날 또는 팔목을 이용하여 물러나면서 막으며, 이 동작 후 곧바로 역습하는 방법입니다.

Words

manner 방식, 태도
order 순서
counter attack 역습
accordingly 부응해서,
 ~에 맞추어

Expressions

according to~ ~에 따라

2. 세 번 겨루기 (얼굴)

사범   세 번 겨루기에서 얼굴을 목표로 하는 것입니다.

3. One-step Kyorugi (Trunk)

Master This is the advanced type of the three-step Kyorugi. One person attacks only once and the other defends and counter attacks simultaneously. For this reason, this movement needs more skill and its speed and accuracy should be perfect.

4. One-step Kyorugi (Face)

Master At the one-step Kyorugi, both partners aim to attack their opponents' face.

3. 한 번 겨루기 (몸통)

사범　세 번 겨루기에서 발전한 형태입니다. 한 사람이 한 번만 공격하기로 약속하고, 상대방은 방어하면서 동시에 바로 반격을 하는 것이죠. 따라서 세 번 겨루기보다 더 숙달이 되어야 하며, 속도와 정확성도 완벽해야 합니다.

4. 한 번 겨루기 (얼굴)

사범　한 번 겨루기에서 얼굴을 목표로 하는 것입니다.

5. Sitting-Position Kyorugi

Master Both partners attack and defend at squatting position. Face Punch is mostly used as an attack technique and Face Blocking, Neck Hit, Front Kick and Side Kick are for the defense.

6. On-the-chair Kyorugi

Master Both partners attack and defend at sitting position. Face Punch is the major attack technique and Neck Hit with both hands and Face Spiral (Turning) Kick are some defense techniques.

5. 앉아 겨루기

사범   같이 쪼그려 앉은 자세에서 공격과 방어를 하는 것입니다. 이때 사용하는 공격 기술은 얼굴지르기이며, 방어는 얼굴막기, 목치기, 앞차기, 옆차기 등입니다.

Words

squat 쪼그려앉다
sit 앉다
major 주요한, 주된
spiral (turning) kick
   돌려차기

6. 의자 겨루기

사범   같이 의자에 앉은 자세에서 공격과 방어를 합니다. 주요 공격 기술은 얼굴지르기이며, 방어 기술은 양손으로 목치기와 얼굴 돌려차기입니다.

7. Types of Person vs. Weapon

Master   The followings are the type of 'person vs weapon'. Namely, it is to learn the defense skill against the opponent armed with weapons such as bar, knife, pistol, and bayonet.

Short–bar Kyorugi

Long–bar Kyorugi

Knife Kyirugu

Sword Kyorugi

Pistol Kyorugi

7. 사람 대 무기 겨루기

사범   다음에 열거되는 겨루기는 '사람 대 무기' 형식입니다. 즉, 상대방이 무기를 들고 공격해 올 때 대처하는 기술을 숙달하고자 하는 것이죠. 무기로는 막대, 칼, 권총, 총검 등이 사용됩니다.

Words

weapon 무기
bar 막대
knife 칼
pistol 권총
bayonet 총검

Expressions

armed with~ ~로 무
장하다

Part 5
Self-Defense

호신술

Master   Hello everyone, how was your summer vacation? Have you been to any good places?

Disciple   Yes, master. We've had a good vacation.

Master   Sounds good. Then let's learn a self-defense briefly at today's first class for the fall semester.

Have any one of you ever heard or learned about a self-defense?

Minsu   Well, isn't it a kind of defense technique to keep safety and protect our body from the other person's threat or attack?

Master   Almost correct. Basically, it is a self-defense technique for our body's safety. Also, it is a self-defense movement against a sudden attack from either one person or a group of people.

Young Ho   What kind of movements are there? Do they refer to such martial arts as Taekwondo, Judo, Hapkido, and so forth?

Master   It includes all of them. Rather, you may recall such basic movements as escaping, throwing, breaking, twist, kick, and hit. These are the techniques of

사범	안녕하세요, 모두 여름방학 잘 보냈습니까? 좋은 곳에 다녀왔나요?
문하생	네, 사범님. 잘 보냈습니다.
사범	좋아요, 그럼 오늘 가을학기 첫 수업에서는 호신술에 대해 간단히 알아보기로 하겠습니다.
사범	여러분 중 호신술에 대해 들어봤거나 배워본 학생 있나요?
민수	글쎄요, 누군가가 우리를 위협하거나 공격할 때 몸의 안전을 도모하고 지키기 위한 방어술이 아닐까요?
사범	기본적으로 우리 몸의 안전을 도모하기 위한 기술이고요, 한 사람 또는 다수의 갑작스런 공격으로부터 자신을 보호하는 동작인거죠.
영호	어떤 종류의 동작이 있는가요? 태권도, 유도, 합기도 등의 무술을 말하는 건가요?
사범	호신술은 그러한 동작들을 모두 포함하죠. 그보다는 기본동작들인 피하기, 메치기, 꺾기, 비틀기, 차기, 치기 등으로 상대방을 제압하기 위한 기술을 떠올리면 됩니다.

Words

summer vacation 여름방학
briefly 간단히
fall semester 가을학기
self-defense 호신술
protect 방어하다
sudden attack 갑작스런 공격
martial art 무예
escaping 피하기
throwin 메치기
breaking 꺾기

overpowering the opponent.

Master   In this regard, on the basis of movements in confrontation, a couple of defense and offense techniques have been developed through some martial arts.

Young Ho   Could you explain it in more details?

Master   Well, on one hand, such types of Taekwondo, Judo and Karate use bare hands for their movements. On the other hand, some other types could use small tools like a nightstick (or police baton).

Master   Also, there are many types of self defense according to its developers from their own ideas or experiences. Thus, we could say the number of self defense techniques is numerous indeed.

Do Hee   Would you explain its techniques to us one by one?

Master   Okay. When it comes to Breaking, it is known as the most efficient method of all. It defensds one's own body by breaking or twisting the opponent's joint of both hands and shoulder as well as wrist.

Master   Hit (or hitting) consists of the fastest and most

사범 그렇기에 필연적으로 대적동작을 중심으로 하여 수비와 공격의 동작을 무술로부터 취하여 만들어진 것이 많아요.

영호 조금 더 자세히 설명해주시겠습니까, 사범님?

사범 음 글쎄요. 덧붙여 말하자면 태권도, 유도, 공수도와 같이 맨손으로 몸동작만을 쓰는 것이 있는가 하면, 경찰봉과 같은 소용구를 사용하는 것도 있다.

사범 또한 발안자의 착상 혹은 체험에 기준하여 발전된 많은 수의 유파가 있습니다. 따라서 호신술의 기술은 무한하다고 볼 수 있습니다.

도희 그럼 몇 가지 기술들을 하나씩 설명해주시겠습니까?

사범 꺾기는 가장 효율적인 방법으로 잘 알려져 있는 기술입니다. 손목 외에도 양팔·어깨관절을 꺾거나 비틀어 내 몸을 보호하는 기술이죠.

사범 치기는 가장 빠르고 간단한 동작으로 이루어집니다. 내 몸이 상대에

Words

overpower 제압하다
nightstick(police baton) 경찰봉
developer 발안자, 개발자
experience 경험
numerous 헤아릴 수 없는
efficient 효과적인
method 기술, 방법

Expressions

in confrontation 대립 상태에 있는
consists of~ ~로 이루어지다, 구성되다

simple movements. When one's body gets caught by the opponent, one could escape hitting the opponent's vital points with the most quick and strong way.

Master   Throwing is not used independently, but as the form of throwing after breaking or throwing after hitting. You may excercise this techinique with your partner.

Disciple   Yes, master.

Master   Throwing uses the power of the incoming opponent and to the axis that one's body turns.

Master   Today, we've learned briefly about a couple of self defense techniques. I hope you can use its skills well in your everyday life.

Disciple   Thanks, master. See you next class.

게 잡혀 있을 때 급소만을 노려 가장 빠르고 강하게 쳐서 빠져나올
수 있는 기술입니다.

사범 던지기에는 주로 꺾은 후 던지기, 친 후 던지기 등이 자주 사용되며,
던지기만을 사용하는 경우는 극히 드물다고 봐도 됩니다. 서로 짝을
이뤄 같이 연습해보기 바랍니다.

문하생 네, 알겠습니다.

사범 던지기는 들어오는 상대의 힘을 이용하여 내가 도는 축으로 상대를
던지는 원리를 사용합니다.

사범 이상 오늘은 간단하게 몇 가지 호신술에 대해 알아보았고요, 실생활
에서 잘 활용하게 되기를 바랍니다.

문하생 감사합니다, 사범님. 다음 수업에서 뵙겠습니다.

Words

vital point 급소
independently 독립적
　으로
axis 축

Expressions

get caught by~ ~에
　게 잡히디
a couple of 두서너 개
　의, 몇 가지의

Part 6
Taekwondo Demonstration Group
태권도시범단

1. What is the Taekwondo Performance Group?

Master   Taekwondo Performance Group literally means a group which shows several performances in front of a group of people. Mainly, they show Poomsae, Kyorugi, Kick(Kicking) and so forth.

They often show demonstration whenever such events as Taekwondo Championships, other special events, and/or the promotion of cultural exchanges among nations are held.

To summarize, Taekwondo Performance Group shows the composite arts of Taekwondo. To explain it concretely, they arrange for basic movements, Poomsae, Kyorugi, breaking, self-defense and acrobatic movements to show these in a short time.

With the naming of 'performance group', the effect of Taekwondo performance has been maximized.

The most representative Korean performance group is 'Kukkiwon Performance Group.' It was founded in 1974 and is now being operated with about 70 group members.

1. 태권도시범단이란?

사범

태권도시범단이란 말 그대로 사람들 앞에서 여러 가지 시범을 보이는 그룹이나 팀을 말합니다. 시범단은 주로 품새, 겨루기, 발차기 등을 보여줍니다.

태권도 시합이나 특별한 대회가 있을 때 또는 다른 나라와 문화교류를 증진할 때 하는 경우가 많습니다.

종합하면 태권도시범단은 태권도의 종합예술을 보여주기 위해 준비된 그룹입니다. 구체적으로 기본동작, 품새, 겨루기, 격파, 호신술, 묘기 등을 구성하여 짧은 시간 내에 보여주게 됩니다.

태권도시범은 '시범단'이란 이름 아래 그 효과가 극대화되어 왔습니다.

한국의 대표적인 시범단은 '국기원시범단'으로 1974년 창단되어 단원 수 약 70명 내외로 운영되고 있습니다.

Words

literally 말 그대로
performance 공연
mainly 주로
demonstration 시범
promotion 증진, 홍보
cultural exchange 문화교류
summarize 요약하다
composite art 종합예술
acrobatic 묘기
maximize 최대화하다
representative 대표적인

Expressions

a group of 일단의
such as ~와 같은
in a short time 짧은 시간 내에

For those of overseas visitors to Korea, the Kukkiwon Perfromance Group has also been proceeding the regular Gyeong-hui-gung Palace performance every week since 2007.

In 2008, Korea Taekwondo Association established their own performance group for the purpose of 'creation of the new performance culture.' Further, World Taekwondo Federation established their own performance group to introduce the superiority of Taekwondo as well as to highlight the image of the federation to the whole world.

Nowadays, a lot of other performance groups have been organized under several colleges and local governments and they are working on positive lines.

Taekwondo Performance Group first aims to get promotion effects for Taekwondo propagation. In addition, they help enhance national prestige via a series of overseas tours.

국기원시범단은 해외 관광객을 위해 경희궁 정기시범을 2007년부터 매주 진행하고 있기도 합니다.

대한태권도협회는 '새로운 시범문화의 창출'을 목표로 하는 시범공연단을 2008년에 창단하였고, 세계태권도연맹 또한 '태권도의 우수성을 전 세계에 알리고 세계연맹의 이미지를 부각시키기 위해' 시범단을 창단했습니다.

현재는 여러 대학과 지방자치단체(시도협회) 산하에 시범단이 구성되어 활발한 활동을 하고 있습니다.

태권도시범단은 일차적으로 태권도 보급을 위해 홍보효과를 얻는 것을 목적으로 하며, 더불어 일련의 해외 순방을 통해서 국위선양에도 기여하고 있습니다.

Words

overseas visitor 해외 관광객
proceed 진행하다
superiority 우월함
highlight 부각시키다
organize 조직하다
propagation 선전

Expressions

as well as ~뿐만 아니라
in addition 더불어
enhance national prestige 국위를 선양하다

2. What is the Taekwondo Performance?

Master   Taekwondo Performance forms one category of technique systems of today's Taekwondo and is still enlarging its boundary.

That is, a Taekwondo trainee shows Taekwondo techniques and acrobatic movements to show people what Taekwondo is and how spectating it is.

Through the performances, people could be curious and interested in it so that it leads people's desire to learn Taekwondo.

Also, Taewondo performers might have pride and self-respect as the Taekwondo trainee through spectating people's praises and cheers.

There have been a couple of changes in the extent and style of Taekwondo performance.

Namely, the artistic value is being added into Taekwondo performance. Thus, Taekwondo performance itself is developing as the style of artistic performance.

2. 태권도시범이란?

사범
태권도시범은 오늘날 태권도의 기술체계의 한 장르를 이루고 있으며, 그 의미가 확장되고 있습니다.

즉, 태권도를 수련한 사람이 태권도 기술과 묘기를 보여줌으로써 보는 사람으로 하여금 태권도가 무엇인가를 알려주게 되죠.

이를 통해 일반인은 신기함과 흥미를 느끼게 되어 배우고자 하는 의욕을 갖게 되는 것입니다.

또한 시범을 보이는 사람은 관람자의 찬사와 환호를 받으며, 태권도인으로서 긍지와 자부심을 갖게 될 것입니다.

태권도시범의 내용과 양식에도 변화가 이어지고 있습니다.

즉, 태권도시범에 예술성이 가미되고 있으며, 이는 예술공연의 형태로 발전되고 있는 것입니다.

Words

category 범주, 장르
enlarge 확장하다
acrobatic 곡예의
spectate 지켜보다
curious 호기심어린
self-respect 자부심
praise 찬사
cheer 환호

Expressions

be interested in~ ~에 흥미를 느끼다

3. The Type and Method of Taekwondo Performance

Master   The types of Taekwondo performance are classified into sole and group performance.

Group performance is again classified into group performance, mass game performance (or group gymnastics performance) and dance performance.

The number of performance group members is about 20 to 30 persons. These trainee personnels show performance by including the general techniques of Taekwondo.

Because such a group size and performance method are the most effective for the promotion to spectators. Such a size and method could be the ideal examples of Taekwondo performance.

Mass game performance was first introduced at the 1st National Youth Games in June of 1972.

As an international event, mass game performance was initially introduced at the opening ceremony of both the 10th 1986 Asian Games and the 24th 1988 Seoul Olympics.

3. 태권도시범의 종류와 방식

사범   태권도 시범의 종류는 단독시범과 단체시범으로 분류됩니다.

단체시범은 다시 시범단 시범, 매스게임 시범, 그리고 무용 시범으로 구분됩니다.

시범단의 규모는 약 20~30명의 요원으로 구성되어 태권도의 전반적인 기술을 총망라하여 시범을 보여줍니다.

왜냐하면 이러한 규모와 방식이 관중들에게 소개하는 데 가장 효과적이며, 태권도시범의 기본이기 때문입니다.

매스게임 시범의 효시는 1972년 6월 제1회 전국소년체육대회 개막식에서 첫 선을 보인 것입니다.

국제행사에서는 1986년 제10회 아시안게임 및 1988년 제24회 서울올림픽 개막식에서 소개된 바 있습니다.

4. How to be a member of National Taekwondo Performance Group

Master   Members for the National Taekwondo Performance Group are recruited.

Some of them are recruited among the candidates from the president of local governments.

Some others are also recruited through a professor's recommendation at the Department of Taekwondo in universities.

Qualifications for the recruitment are as follows:

- Aged over 19
- Academic Achievement of High School
- Holder of Certificate of Kukkiwon Dan(or Poom)
- Winner at the International Championship Tournament
- No Reasons for Disqualification for Overseas Travel
- One Who can train Every Saturday
- One Who can participate in either National or International Performance Event

4. 국가대표 태권도시범단원이 되려면?

사범   국가대표 태권도시범단의 단원은 모집을 통해 채용됩니다.

단원의 일부는 지방자치단체(시도지사 등)의 장이 추천하는 후보들 중에서 채용됩니다.

또한 일부는 대학교 태권도학과 학생 중에서 교수의 추천으로 모집되기도 합니다.

응시자격은 다음과 같습니다:

- 만 19세 이상
- 고등학교 졸업 이상 학력
- 국기원 단(品)증 소지자
- 국제경기 우승자
- 해외여행 결격사유가 없는 자
- 매주 토요일 훈련이 가능한 자
- 국내외 시범행사에 참가할 수 있는 자

Words

recruite 모집하다
candidate 후보자
professor 교수
recommendation 추천
qualification 자격
disqualification 결격,
  불합격

Expressions

participate in~ ~에
  참가하다

In case of regular recruitment, the contents of candidate's performance are as follows:

- Demonstration of Synthesized Breaking
- Demonstraoin of Power Breaking
- Breaking with Accuracy
- High Jumping Kick
- Overstepping Kick against Obstacle at a Distance
- Self Defense Martial Arts
- Kyorugi at a Match
- Usage of Weaponry

Besides the performance contents mentioned above, the mandatory (or required) subjects for all candidates are as follows:

- Basic Physical Fitness including Muscular Strength, Quickness, Ability to reack instantly, Flexibility, Cardiopulmonary Endurance
- Basic Hand and Foot Movements
- Poomsae including Koryo, Pyongwon, Sipjin, Jitae

Furthermore, candidates may select either specialty or free item as their optional subject.

If there is not any proper candidate at all as for the contents of performances, not a single candidate

정규 모집의 경우 후보자의 시범내용은 다음과 같이 구성됩니다.

- 종합격파
- 위력격파
- 정확성 격파
- 높이뛰어차기
- 멀리장애물 넘어차기
- 호신술
- 경기겨루기
- 무기술

위 구성내용 외에 후보자 모두에게 요구되는 필수종목은 다음과 같습니다:

- 기초체력 : 근력, 민첩성, 순발력, 유연성, 심폐지구력 등
- 기본동작 : 손동작, 발동작
- 품새 : 고려, 평원, 십진, 지태

또한 후보자는 각자 특기종목이나 자유종목을 선택할 수 있습니다.

시범 구성내용을 참고하여 적격자가 없을 경우 선발하지 않을 수도 있습니다.

Words

regular 정규의
content 내용
synthesized 종합적인
obstacle 장애물
weaponry 무기
mandatory 의무적인
quickness 민첩성
flexibility 유연성
cardiopulmonary
  endurance 심폐지구력
specialty 특기, 장기

Expressions

in case of ~의 경우에

could be selected.

If anyone would want to be the member of Taekwondo Performance Group, one may apply for the Department of Taekwondo at a university.

Although it is not a must that one should go to the Department of Taekwondo, it is recommended in that one could be recruited as a member of national team along with career of university Taekwondo performance group.

Above all, Taekwondo trainees may well study for learning's sake as a student.

만약 태권도시범단원이 되고자 한다면 대학교 태권도학과로 진학하는 것이 좋습니다.

꼭 대학교 태권도학과를 가야만 하는 건 아니지만, 일반적으로 대학에서 시범단 생활을 하다 국가대표로 선발되는 경우가 많기 때문입니다.

무엇보다 학생으로서 열심히 공부하며 운동하는 것이 가장 바람직합니다.

Words

recommend 권장하다
career 경력, 이력
trainee 수련자

Expressions

apply for~ ~에 지원하다

Supplement

부록

I. Warm-up Exercises

1.1 Breathing

Master Good morning everyone. It is really a fine day today!

Before proceeding to main exercises, we will learn about the basics of breathing.

Breathing is the act or process of taking air into your lungs and releasing it.

Meantime, breathing takes key roles in maintaining health and correct exercises.

For this reason, let us know about the importance of breathing and some of its methods.

Please listen carefully and follow my actions.

1.1.1 The Importance of Breathing

During stressful situations, we rarely stop to think about what is happening within our bodies.

1. 준비운동

1.1 호흡

사범   좋은 아침입니다. 오늘 날씨가 아주 상쾌하네요!

오늘은 수련에 앞서 호흡에 대해 알아보겠습니다.

호흡이란 숨을 들이마시고 내쉬는 과정을 말합니다.

그런데 호흡은 건강유지와 올바른 운동을 위해 중요한 기능을 수행합니다.

따라서 호흡의 중요성과 몇 가지 호흡법에 대해 알아보도록 하겠습니다.

설명을 들으며 같이 따라하기 바랍니다.

1.1.1 호흡의 중요성

사범   우리는 스트레스를 받는 상황에서 우리 몸에 어떤 변화가 일어나는지 간과하기 쉽습니다.

Words

breathing 호흡
lung 폐
importance 중요성
stressful 스트레스를
받는

Expressions

take key roles in~ ~에
중요한 기능을 하다

Indeed, the pressures of the moments keep our minds occupied on almost everything but our physiological functions.

Consequently, those functions often become irregular, leaving us in an unhealthy state of being.

When we are in this state we have fewer chances to succeed in whatever we try to accomplish.

Among the many physiological functions adversely affected by stress is our breathing.

Even when stress is minimal few people retain a habit of natural and full breathing.

Proper breathing is essential for sustaining life and cleansing inner body systems.

By learning proper breathing techniques stressful situations may be handled better and overall mental and physical health will be improved.

 1.1.2 Proper Breathing Method

Master   Lie down on a rug or blanket on the floor with your legs straight and slightly apart, your toes pointed

실제로, 압박을 받는 순간에 우리의 마음은 생리적인 자연 현상을 제외하곤 무언가에 사로잡히게 됩니다.

그렇게 되면 생리적인 자연적 기능들도 불규칙하게 되고, 건강하지 않은 상황에 놓이게 합니다.

이러한 상태에 놓이게 되면 우리는 무엇을 하려고 해도 제대로 하는 경우가 드물게 되는 것이죠.

스트레스에 의해 부정적인 영향을 받게 되는 여러 생리적 기능들 중의 하나가 호흡입니다.

설령 스트레스가 적은 경우에도 일부 소수의 사람들만이 자연적이고 제대로 된 호흡을 하고 있습니다.

적절한 호흡은 삶을 유지하고 체내시스템을 맑게 하는데 필수적이라 할 수 있습니다.

적절한 호흡 기술을 배움으로써 스트레스 상황에 보다 잘 조절하고 정신 및 신체건강이 좋아질 것입니다.

1.1.2 정상 호흡법

사범 바닥에 담요 위에 누워서 발을 살짝 벌려 뻗으며, 발끝은 바깥으로 향하게 하며, 양팔은 몸에 닿지 않게 옆에 두고, 손바닥은 위로 향하

Words

pressure 압박
physiological 생리적인
function 기능
consequently 그 결과, 따라서
irregular 불규칙한
accomplish 완수하다, 해내다
adversely 불리하게, 반대로
sustain 유지하다
handle 다루다
blanket 담요

Expressions

be essential for~ ~에 필수적이다

comfortably outwards, arms at your sides not touching your body, your palms up, and your eyes closed.

This is called a 'relaxed body' position. Take time to relax your body and breathe freely.

It is best to breathe through your nose, as the tiny hairs and mucous membranes filter out dust and toxins from the inhaled air.

Keep your mouth closed as you breathe. As you breathe, your chest and abdomen should move together.

If only the chest seems to rise and fall, your breathing is shallow and you are not making good use of the lower part of your lungs.

As you inhale you should feel your abdomen rising; it is as if your stomach is filling with air.

As you exhale, the abdomen comes back in, like a balloon releasing all its air.

This inhale and exhale process should continue comfortably and smoothly.

게 하고, 눈을 감습니다.

이것을 편한 몸의 자세라고 합니다. 몸의 긴장을 풀게 하고 편하게 숨을 쉬어봅니다.

코털과 점막이 유입된 공기에 있는 먼지와 독소를 걸러낼 때에 코를 통해 숨을 쉬는 것이 가장 좋습니다.

숨을 쉴 때는 입을 다뭅니다. 동시에 가슴과 복부가 같이 움직여야 합니다.

만약 가슴만 위아래로 움직인다면 호흡을 깊게 한 것이 아니라서 폐의 아래 부위를 제대로 사용하지 못하고 있는 것입니다.

숨을 들이킬 때 마치 위가 공기로 가득한 것처럼 당신의 복부가 부풀어 올라야 합니다.

숨을 내쉴 때 풍선이 바람을 모두 빼는 것처럼 복부는 다시 내려와야 합니다.

이러한 흡입과 내쉼이 편하고 부드럽게 계속되어야 합니다.

Words

comfortably 편한하게
freely 자유롭게
mucous 먼지
toxin 독소
inhale 들이쉬다
abdomen 배
shallow 얕은
stomach 위

Expressions

keep closed 닫힌 채를 유지하다

1.1.3 Deep, Relaxed Breathing

Master   Although this exercise can be practiced in a variety of poses, the following is recommended for beginners:

Lie down on a blanket or rug on the floor. Bend your knees and move your feet about eight inches apart, with your toes turned outward slightly. Make sure your spine is straight.

Place one hand on your abdomen and the other hand on your chest.

Inhale slowly and deeply through your nose into your abdomen to push up your hand as much as feels comfortable. Your chest should move only a little and only with your abdomen.

Continue step three until it becomes rhythmic and comfortable. Now smile slightly, inhale through your nose and exhale through your mouth, make a quiet and breezy sound as you gently blow out.

Your mouth, tongue and jaw will be relaxed. Take long, slow, deep breaths raising and lowering your abdomen. Hear the sound and feel the texture of breathing as you become more and more relaxed.

1.1.3 심호흡, 이완호흡법

사범   이 방법은 다양한 형태로 수행할 수 있으나 초보자는 다음의 방식으로 할 것을 권합니다.

바닥의 담요 위에 눕습니다. 무릎을 굽히고 양 발을 20cm 정도 서로 떨어뜨리며, 발끝이 바깥으로 살짝 향하게 합니다. 이때 척추(등뼈)가 일자가 되도록 펴야 합니다.

한 손은 복부에 얹고, 다른 손은 가슴에 얹습니다.

손이 최대한 편하게 내려가도록 코를 통해서 복부로 천천히 그리고 깊게 숨을 들이마십니다.

위의 단계가 자연스럽고 편하게 될 때까지 반복합니다. 이제 살짝 미소를 지으며 코를 통해 들이마시고 입을 통해 내쉬며, 조용하고 산들바람이 부는 듯이 소리를 내 봅니다.

입, 혀, 턱이 편해질 것입니다. 복부를 올렸다 내렸다 하면서 길고 천천히 숨을 깊게 쉽니다. 더욱 편하게 이완될 때 호흡의 소리와 원리를 느껴보세요.

Words

comfortable 편안한
rhythmic 리드미컬한, 율동적인
tongue 혀

Expressions

make sure 확인하다
blow out (바람이) 불다

When you first begin this technique, do it for five minutes. When you become more comfortable with it, you may extend it up to 20 minutes.

Upon ending a session, stay still for a few minutes and try to keep the entire body relaxed.

1.2 Stretching

1.2-1.2.3

Master Next, let us learn about stretching which is done right before main exercises.

1.2.1 Why stretch?

Master Stretching is useful for both injury prevention and injury treatment.

For the purposes of this session I will concentrate on prevention.

If done properly, stretching increases flexibility and this directly translates into reduced risk of injury.

The reason is that a muscle/tendon group with a greater range of motion passively will be less likely to experience tears when used actively.

이 기술을 처음 사용하는 경우라면 5분간 반복하기 바랍니다. 더 편해지면 시간을 20분으로 늘려도 좋습니다.

이 방식으로 호흡을 마치면 몇 분간 그대로 있으며 몸 전체가 이완되도록 유지해봅니다.

1.2 스트레칭

사범   자, 그럼 다음으로 운동 전 스트레칭에 대해 알아보겠습니다.

1.2.1 스트레칭을 하는 이유?

사범   스트레칭은 상해예방과 부상치료에 효과적으로 이용합니다.

이번 수업의 목적에 맞게 저는 상해예방에 초점을 맞춰 설명하겠습니다.

만약 제대로 하신다면, 스트레칭은 유연성을 높이고 부상의 위험을 직접적으로 줄이게 되는 효과가 있습니다.

그 이유는 큰 모션을 취하게 되는 근육/힘줄의 경우 제대로 잘 사용되면 통증을 적게 느낄 수 있기 때문입니다.

Words

entire 모든, 전부의
injury prevention 상해
  예방
treatment 치료
concentrate 집중하다
experience 경험하다

Expressions

learn about~ ~을 배
  우다
for the purposes of~
  ~을 위하여

Stretching is also thought to improve recovery and may enhance athletic performance.

The latter has not been fully agreed upon in the medical literature, but improved bio-mechanical efficiency has been suggested as an explanation.

Additionally, increased flexibility of the neck, shoulders and upper back may improve respiratory function.

1.2.2 How to stretch?

Master   There are three methods of stretching: static, ballistic (bouncing), and proprioceptive neuromuscular facilitation (PNF).

Static is the method recommended for the majority of athletes since it is the least likely to cause injury.

Ballistic(bouncing) and PNF stretching are probably best reserved for a select few who are experienced with their use.

To get the most benefit from your static stretching routine while minimizing injury, stretching should be done after warm-up exercises.

스트레칭은 또한 (운동 후) 회복에 도움을 주고 운동능력을 향상시키는 것으로 여겨집니다.

후자의 경우(운동능력 향상) 의학계에서 아직 공통된 견해가 있지는 않으나, 향상된 생체역학적인 효능이 대안으로 제시되고 있습니다.

부가적으로, 목/어깨/등 위쪽의 유연성이 향상되면 순환기능이 좋아진다고 합니다.

1.2.2 스트레칭 방법

사범   스트레칭은 세 가지로 구분 됩니다 : 정적, 탄력, PNF

정적 스트레칭은 부상을 가장 적게 일으키기 때문에 대부분의 운동선수들에게 추천되는 방식입니다.

탄력 및 PNF 스트레칭은 그 사용법에 경험 있는 소수를 위해 준비된 것입니다.

부상을 최소화하며 정적 스트레칭 중에 최대한의 효과를 얻기 위해서는 반드시 준비운동을 해야 합니다.

Words

recovery 회복
athletic performance
 운동능력
bio-mechanical 생체
 역학적인
efficiency 효능
respiratory function
 호흡기능
static 정적
ballistic 탄력적
minimize 최소화하다

Expressions

likely to~ ~하기 위운
get benefit from~ ~
로붙 이득을 얻다

Gaining from warm-up exercises, the increased blood flow to the muscles aids in the flexibility and is an important component for injury prevention.

Static stretching is done by slowly moving a joint towards its end-range of motion.

A gentle 'pulling' sensation should be felt in the desired muscle. This position is then held for 15 - 20 seconds.

Do not stretch to the point of pain and do not bounce since this may cause injury to the muscle. Within a session, each subsequent stretch of a particular muscle group seems to give progressively more flexibility.

A set of 3 to 5 stretches is probably sufficient to get the maximum out of the routine. It is also a good idea to start with the neck and progress down to the feet.

This enables you to take advantage of gains in flexibility from the previously stretched muscle groups. Stretching should also be done after the workout.

준비운동을 통해서 얻어진 근육 내에 증가한 혈류는 유연성에도 도움을 주고 부상방지에도 중요한 요소가 됩니다.

정적 스트레칭은 관절을 움직일 수 있는 가장 큰 범위까지 천천히 옮기면서 하면 됩니다.

(스트레칭으로 인해) 기대하는 근육부위에 부드럽게 끌어당겨지는 감각이 느껴져야 합니다. 이 자세가 15 내지 20초 동안 유지되도록 합니다.

아픈 부위로 스트레칭하면 안되며, 뛰는 것도 근육에 부상을 일으킬 수 있으니 삼가야 합니다. 스트레칭 중에 특정 근육의 연속된 세부 스트레치는 점진적인 유연성을 키워줍니다.

일상에서 3 내지 5개의 스트레치 동작 정도면 최고의 효과를 얻기에 충분할 것입니다. 목부터 시작해서 발 아래쪽으로 내려가는 것이 좋은 방식입니다.

이러한 방식은 당신이 이전에 스트레치했던 근육 부위와 함께 더 유연성을 키우게 해 줄 것입니다.

Words

flexibility 유연성
component 구성요소
subsequent 그 다음,
  차후의
previously 이전에 , 미리

Expressions

take advantage of~
  ~의 효과를 얻다

The post-workout stretch is thought to aid in recovery. Cold packs can be applied to sore areas in those of you who are recovering from injuries.

1.2.3 Tips for Stretching

Master Stretch at least three times a week to maintain flexibility.

A session should last 10 to 20 minutes, with each static stretch held at least 10 seconds (working up to 20 to 30 seconds) and usually repeated about four times.

Stretch before exercising or playing a sport to improve performance and perhaps prevent injury.

Besides a general stretch of major muscle groups, stretch the specific muscles required for your sport or activity.

Don't bounce. Stretching should be gradual and relaxed.

Focus on the muscle groups you want to stretch.

실전 스트레치 이후는 회복에 도움을 준다고 합니다. 부상에서 회복 중인 사람에게는 통증 부위에 차가운 팩을 해주면 좋습니다.

1.2.3 스트레칭 시의 주의사항

사범 유연성을 유지하기 위해서 일주일에 최소 3회 스트레치 합니다.

한 회는 최소 10 내지 20분 동안 해야 하며, 개별 정적 스트레치는 최소 10초로 하여(점차 20 내지 30초로 증가) 대개 네 번 정도 반복합니다.

운동 또는 스포츠경기 직전에 하여 실전에서 더 잘하고 부상 방지에도 도움을 주게 합니다.

주요 근육 부위에 일상적인 스트레칭을 하며, 어떠한 스포츠 종목이나 활동에 필수적으로 사용되는 특정 근육에도 마찬가지로 합니다.

뛰지 않는 것이 좋습니다. 스트레칭은 점진적이고도 이완이 되도록 해야 합니다.

스트레치하고자 하는 근육 부위에 집중해도 좋습니다.

Words

recovery 회복
maintain 유지하다
repeat 반복하다
besides ~외에도
bounce (깡총깡총) 뛰다, 튀다
gradual 서서히, 점진적인

Expressions

focus on~ ~에 집중하다

Try to stretch opposing muscles in both your arms and legs. Include static stretches plus PNF.

Don't hold your breath while stretching.

Stretch after exercising to prevent muscles from tightening up.

팔과 다리에 있는 대비되는 근육들을 스트레치해보세요. 정적 또는
PNF 스트레칭을 가미해보세요.

스트레치 중에 호흡을 멈추지 말아야 합니다.

운동 후에도 근육이 뭉치지 않기 위해 스트레치를 합니다.

Words

oppose 반대하다, 겨루다
include 포함하다

Expressions

hold breath 숨을 참다
prevent from~ ~하는 것을 방지하다

2. English Conversation in Taekwondo

🎧 `conversation 1` Conversation 1

Min Soo   Hello, Young Ho!

Young Ho   Hi, Min Soo!

Min Soo   How are you today!

Young Ho   I'm fine, thank you. And you?

Min Soo   Very good. I started learning Taekwondo two weeks ago.

Young Ho   Oh, really? Are you enjoying it?

Min Soo   It is awesome. It really makes my body and mind healthy. You can join me if you like!

Young Ho   I'll pass, thank you.

2. 태권도 영어 회화

Words

awesome 기막히게 좋
은, 굉장한
join 참가하다

회화 1

민수 영호야 안녕!

영호 안녕 민수야!

민수 오늘 기분 어떠니?

영호 응, 난 좋아, 넌 어때?

민수 아주 좋아~ 나 2주 전에 태권도 배우기 시작했어.

영호 정말? 배울만하니?

민수 응 끝내줘~ 태권도를 배우니까 내 몸과 마음이 건강해지는 것 같아.

　　　너도 괜찮으면 같이 배우자!

영호 난 괜찮아, 고마워.

🎧 `conversation 2` Conversation 2

Min Soo   What's your hobby, Young Ho?

Young Ho   I like exercising Taekwondo very much.

Min Soo   Oh, it looks nice. Where do you exercise it?

Young Ho   In a Taekwondo studio near my house.

Min Soo   How often are you exercising it? Aren't you tired?

Young Ho   No, it's adorably worthy of training. Would you like to join me? You will really love it!

Young Ho   Well, I'm not sure I can do it. Let me think about it and get back to you soon.

🎧 `conversation 3` Conversation 3

Min Soo   What's your favorite kicking, Young Ho?

Young Ho   My favorite kicking is Front Kick.

Min Soo   Are you good at Front Kick?

Young Ho   Sure, I am really good at Front Kick.

Min Soo   Then, what do you think of your week point in your Front Kick skill?

Young Ho   I think I need more exact movements!

회화 2

민수 영호야 넌 취미가 뭐니?

영호 응 나는 태권도 운동하는 것을 굉장히 좋아해.

민수 와, 그거 좋아 보인다. 어디에서 운동하니?

영호 집 근처에 있는 태권도장에서 해.

민수 얼마나 자주 하니? 힘들지 않니?

영호 전혀~ 정말 운동할만한 가치가 많아. 너도 나랑 같이 할래? 너도 분명 많이 좋아하게 될 거야!

민수 글쎄, 내가 잘 할 수 있을지 확신이 서지 않아. 생각해보고 나중에 다시 알려줄게.

회화 3

민수 영호야, 너는 발차기 기술 중에 어떤 것을 선호하니?

영호 내가 좋아하는 것은 앞차기야.

민수 앞차기 잘하니?

영호 물론이지, 나는 앞차기는 정말 잘해.

민수 그럼 너의 앞차기 기술에서 약점은 무엇이라고 생각해?

영호 내 생각에 나는 조금 더 정확하게 차야할 것 같아!

Words

hobby 취미
adorably 정말로, 경탄할 만큼
favorite 좋아하는
exact 정확한

Expressions

worthy of~ ~할 가치가 있는

▶ conversation 4 Conversation 4

Min Soo   Can you do any martial arts, Young Ho?

Young Ho   One of the oriental martial arts, Taekwondo.

Min Soo   What rank are you in Taekwondo?

Young Ho   I'm not a beginner and my belt is brown.

Min Soo   How long have you been exercising to get brown?

Young Ho   Not that long beyond my expectations, say, about two months?

▶ conversation 5 Conversation 5

Min Soo   Have you finished learning trunk opposite punch this month, Young Ho?

Young Ho   Yes, I've already finished.

Min Soo   I've still got a lot to learn. It's too difficult for me.

Young Ho   Do you need my help?

Min Soo   Yes, I'll appreciate it if you help me.

Young Ho   No problem. What's the most difficult part to you?

회화 4

민수   영호야, 너 무술 할 수 있는 것 있니?

영호   동아시아의 전통 무예들 중의 하나인 태권도 할 수 있어.

민수   태권도 단급이 무엇이니?

영호   초보자는 아니고 갈색 띠야.

민수   갈색 띠 얻기까지 얼마나 걸렸니?

영호   내 예상에 비해 그리 오래 걸리지는 않았어. 아마 약 두 달 정도.

회화 5

민수   영호야, 너 이번 달에 몸통반대지르기 배우는 것 마쳤니?

영호   응, 벌써 끝냈어.

민수   나는 아직 배워야 할 것이 많아. 나에게는 너무 어려운 것 같아.

영호   내가 도와줄까?

민수   응. 그래주면 너무 고맙겠어.

영호   천만에. 너에게 가장 어려운 부분이 무엇이니?

Words

martial art 무예
oriental 동양의
rank 급수, 단급
beginner 초보자
belt 띠
brown 갈색
appreciate 고마워하다

Expressions

beyond expectations
예상밖으로

Conversation 6

Min Soo	Young Ho, do you know why Tae Jin is absent from the Taekwondo class today?
Young Ho	I've heard that he's in the hospital.
Min Soo	Oh, really? What happened with him in the world?
Young Ho	He missed his step so got seriously injured during exercise at home.
Min Soo	How did you get to know it?
Young Ho	His mother called me this morning.
Min Soo	I see. Why don't we go see him after class?
Young Ho	Sure.

Conversation 7

Instructor	Aren't you tired? Let's take a ten-minute break.
Students	Thank you.
Instructor	(A few minutes later) Everyone, gather around.
Student 1	Pardon?
Student 2	Has the break finished already?
Instructor	How many minutes have passed?
Student 3	Just five minutes, sir
Instructor	Sorry, then let's take five minutes more.

회화 6

민수	영호야, 너 태진이가 오늘 태권도 수업에 왜 결석한 것인지 아니?
영호	태진이가 병원에 있다고 들었어.
민수	아, 정말? 도대체 태진에게 무슨 일이 생긴 거야?
영호	집에서 운동하던 중에 발을 헛디뎌서 심하게 다쳤대.
민수	너는 그것을 어떻게 아는 거니?
영호	태진 어머니께서 오늘 아침에 전화해주셨어.
민수	그렇구나. 수업 끝나고 태진에게 같이 가볼까?
영호	좋아, 그러자.

Words

absent 결석한
hospital 병원
seriously 심하게

Expressions

miss one's step 발을 헛딛다

회화 7

강사	힘들지 않은가요? 10분간 휴식을 갖도록 하죠.
학생들	감사합니다.
강사	(몇 분 후에) 여러분, 모여주세요.
학생 1	네?
학생 2	벌써 휴식시간이 지난 건가요?
강사	몇 분 지났죠?
학생 3	이제 5분 지났습니다, 사범님.
강사	미안합니다. 그럼 5분 더 쉬도록 하겠습니다.

🎧 conversation 8 Conversation 8

Min Soo	What happened, Young Ho?
Young Ho	I sprained my ankle yesterday.
Min Soo	Are you okay?
Young Ho	I think I can not exercise Taekwondo for a while.
Min Soo	Why don't you go to see a doctor?
Young Ho	I made an appointment for tomorrow.
Min Soo	Hope you will be good.
Young Ho	I also hope it's not a serious injury.

🎧 conversation 9 Conversation 9

Min Soo	I'm so stressed out.
Young Ho	What's wrong with you, Min Su?
Min Soo	I'm (getting) tired of learning Taekwondo these days.
Young Ho	Don't worry, just enjoy it!
Min Soo	Young Ho, let's go to the taekwondo hall together.
Young Ho	That's a good idea. Let's try to get rid of stress (by) exercising Taekwondo together.

회화 8

민수   영호야, 무슨 일 있었니?

영호   어제 발목을 삐었어.

민수   괜찮니?

영호   내 생각에 한동안 태권도 연습하지 못할 것 같아.

민수   의사에게 가서 보이지 그러니?

영호   내일 만나기로 예약해놨어.

민수   별일 없기를 바랄께.

영호   나도 큰 부상이 아니길 바라고 있어.

Words

injury 부상, 상해
appointment 약속

회화 9

민수   나 너무 스트레스 받았어.

영호   민수야, 뭐가 문제니?

민수   요즘 태권도 배우는 것이 점점 힘들어지고 있어.

영호   걱정 하지 마, 그냥 즐겨!

민수   영호야, 나랑 같이 태권도장에 다니자.

영호   좋은 생각이야. 같이 태권도 배우면서 스트레스를 없애도록 노력
            해보자.

Expressions

sprain ankle 발목을 삐
  끗하다
for a while 한동안
get rid of~ ~을 없애다

🎧 `conversation 10` Conversation 10

Instructor	Let's learn a new way of kicking, students.
Students	Yes, master!
Instructor	Today, you're going to learn how to jump high and kick toward the front.
Students	Isn't it too difficult?
Instructor	It's easy. Never mind. You can do it.
Students	Okay, we'll try. Please show it to us then.

회화 10

강사	학생들. 오늘은 새로운 차기 방법을 배우겠습니다.
학생들	네, 사범님!
강사	오늘 여러분들은 높이뛰어앞차기 하는 법을 배울 것입니다.
학생들	너무 어려운 것 아닌가요?
강사	쉽습니다. 전혀 걱정하지 마세요. 여러분들은 할 수 있습니다.
학생들	네, 그럼 노력해보겠습니다. 그럼 어떻게 하는 것인지 시범을 보여주십시오.

Words

jump high 높이 뛰다

Expressions

never mind 걱정하지 마라

Index of Taekwondo Terminology

손끝아래젖혀찌르기 Hand Tip Low
Bending Backward Thrusting
손끝엎어찌르기 Hand Tip Downward
Thrusting
손날 Hand Blade
손날금강막기 Hand Blade Diamond
Blocking
손날등 Hand Blade Back
손날등몸통헤쳐막기 Hand Blade Back
Trunk Scattered Blocking
손날바깥치기 Hand Blade Outer Hit
손날비틀어막기 Hand Blade Twist Blocking
손날아래헤쳐막기 Hand Blade Low
Scattered Blocking
손날앞치기 Hand Blade Front Hit
손등 Hand Back
손바닥 Palm
손바닥거들어몸통막기 Palm-assisted Trunk
Blocking

【아】

아금손 Arc Hand
아금손얼굴앞치기[=칼재비] Arc Hand Face
Front Hit [=Kaljebi]
아래 Lower Part of the Body, Low, Beneath
아래내려치기 Low Downward Hit
아래반대세워지르기 Low(Underneath)
Opposite Erected(Vertical) Punch
아래옆차기 Low Side Kick
아래젖혀찌르기 Low Bending Backward
Thrusting

아래지르기 Low(Underneath) Punch
아래표적치기 Low Target Hit
아래헤쳐막기 Low Scattered Blocking
안막기 Inner Blocking
안쫑서기 Inward Stance
안쫑주춤서기 Inward Riding Stance
안차기 Inner Kick
안팔목 Inner Wrist
안팔목거들어바깥막기 Inner Wrist Assisted
Trunk Outer Blocking
안팔목바깥막기 Inner Wrist Trunk Outer
Blocking
안팔목헤쳐막기 Inner Wrist Trunk
Scattered Blocking
앞굽이 Forward Inflection Stance
앞꼬아서기 Forward Cross(Twist) Stance
앞서기 Forward Stance
앞주춤서기 Forward Riding Stance
앞차고돌려차기 Fronk Kick and Spiral
(Turning) Kick
앞차고옆차기 Front Kick and Side Kick
앞차기 Front Kick
앞축 Fore Sole
앞축모아서기 Reverse Attention Stance
앞치기 Forward(Front) Hit
얼굴 Face
얼굴돌려차기 Face Spiral(Turning) Kick
얼굴바깥막기 Face Outer Blocking
얼굴바깥치기 Face Outer Hit
얼굴바로돌려지르기 Face Straight Spiral
(Turning) Punch
얼굴바로지르기 Face Straight Punch

【하】